WILBARGER
WICHITA
BAYLOR
ARCHER
CLAY
MONTAGUE
THROCKMORTON
SHACKELFORD
CALLAHAN
BROWN
COLEMAN
McCULLOCH
SAN SABA
MASON
GILLESPIE
BANDERA
MEDINA
COMAL
GUADALUPE
GONZALES
LAVACA
WILSON
DEWITT
KARNES
FRIO
ATASCOSA
LA SALLE
McMULLEN
LIVE OAK
GOLIAD
VICTORIA
BEE
COLORADO
JACKSON
WHARTON
BRAZORIA
CALDWELL
HOPKINS
RAINS
ROCKWALL
DALLAS
KAUFMAN
VAN ZANDT
HENDERSON
ANDERSON
FREESTONE
LIMESTONE
LEON
MADISON
ROBERTSON
FRANKLIN
BOSQUE
JOHNSON
SOMERVELL
HOOD
CORYELL
BELL
BELTON
CAMERON
WACO
HILLSBORO
CLEBURNE
GRANBURY
WEATHERFORD
FT. WORTH
GREENVILLE
SULPHUR SPRINGS
EMORY
PALESTINE
CROCKETT
HOUSTON
MADISONVILLE
WALKER
MERIDIAN
GROESBECK
COOPER
BOWIE
PANOLA
TYLER
GALVESTON
ATOKA
LAWTON
FREDERICK
RED RIVER
O
M
A
G
U
L
F
O
F
M
E
X
I
C
O

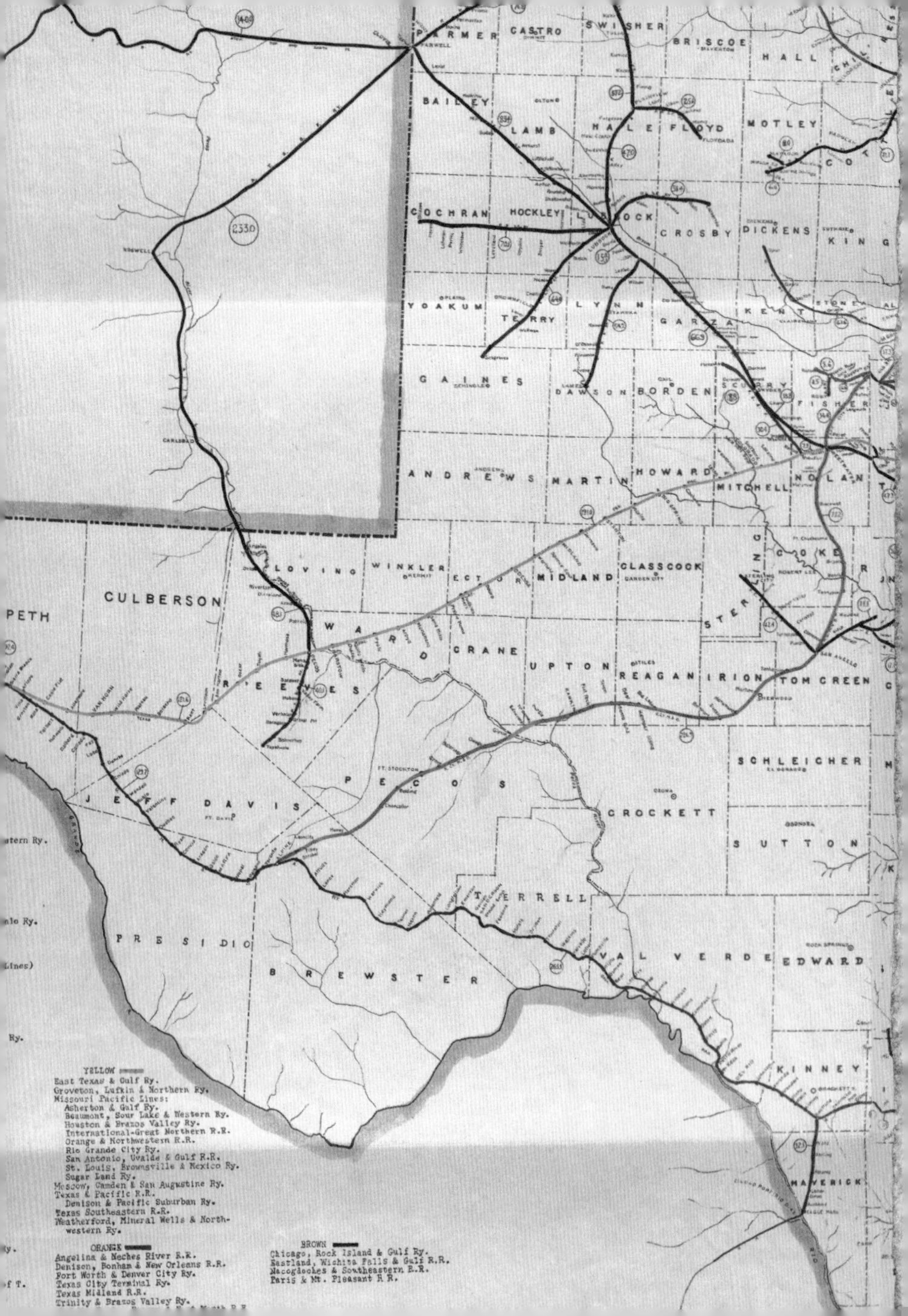
PARMER
CASTRO
SWISHER
BRISCOE
HALL
BAILEY
LAMB
HALE
FLOYD
MOTLEY
COCHRAN
HOCKLEY
LUBBOCK
CROSBY
DICKENS
KING
YOAKUM
TERRY
LYNN
GARZA
KENT
STONEWALL
GAINES
DAWSON
BORDEN
SCURRY
FISHER
ANDREWS
MARTIN
HOWARD
MITCHELL
NOLAN
LOVING
WINKLER
ECTOR
MIDLAND
GLASSCOCK
STERLING
COKE
CULBERSON
WARD
CRANE
UPTON
REAGAN
IRION
TOM GREEN
REEVES
SCHLEICHER
JEFF DAVIS
PECOS
CROCKETT
SUTTON
TERRELL
PRESIDIO
BREWSTER
VAL VERDE
EDWARDS
KINNEY
MAVERICK
CARLSBAD
FT. STOCKTON
SAN ANGELO
YELLOW
East Texas & Gulf Ry.
Groveton, Lufkin & Northern Ry.
Missouri Pacific Lines:
Asherton & Gulf Ry.
Beaumont, Sour Lake & Western Ry.
Houston & Brazos Valley Ry.
International-Great Northern R.R.
Orange & Northwestern R.R.
Rio Grande City Ry.
San Antonio, Uvalde & Gulf R.R.
St. Louis, Brownsville & Mexico Ry.
Sugar Land Ry.
Moscow, Camden & San Augustine Ry.
Texas & Pacific R.R.
Denison & Pacific Suburban Ry.
Texas Southeastern R.R.
Weatherford, Mineral Wells & Northwestern Ry.
ORANGE
Angelina & Neches River R.R.
Denison, Bonham & New Orleans R.R.
Fort Worth & Denver City Ry.
Texas City Terminal Ry.
Texas Midland R.R.
Trinity & Brazos Valley Ry.
BROWN
Chicago, Rock Island & Gulf Ry.
Eastland, Wichita Falls & Gulf R.R.
Nacogdoches & Southeastern R.R.
Paris & Mt. Pleasant R.R.

TEXAS Cocktails

2ND EDITION

AN ELEGANT COLLECTION OF OVER 100 RECIPES INSPIRED BY THE LONE STAR STATE

NICO MARTINI

CIDER MILL PRESS
BOOK PUBLISHERS

Texas Cocktails, 2nd Edition

13-Digit ISBN: 978-1-64643-089-5
10-Digit ISBN: 1-64643-089-1

This book may be ordered by mail from the publisher. Please include $5.99 for postage and handling. Please support your local bookseller first!
Books published by Cider Mill Press Book Publishers are available at special discounts for bulk purchases in the United States by corporations, institutions, and other organizations. For more information, please contact the publisher.

Cider Mill Press Book Publishers
"Where good books are ready for press"
501 Nelson Place
Nashville, TN 37214

cidermillpress.com

Typography: Avenir, Brothers, Copperplate, Sackers, Warnock
Image Credits: see page 365–366

Printed in Malaysia

24 25 26 27 28 SEM 8 7 6 5 4

CONTENTS

—Foreword—

When I began writing about drinks and covering bars and bartenders in Texas twelve years ago, the gig was about finding the places and people doing notable work. Establishments stocking esoteric liqueurs, making their own syrups, and squeezing fresh juices each day were enough to warrant a story. Hell, put your bartenders in fedoras and vests (a uniform that I, too, donned as a part-time bartender many years ago) and you were likely to get your picture in the news. Today, finding worthy bars and drinks to cover isn't the challenge—Texas has both in droves. Instead, it's curation over discovery. It's choosing what and who to highlight and understanding where they fall in the greater industry landscape. It's knowing that you probably missed a couple deserving places along the way, partly because it's a crowded category and partly because new spots pop up faster than you can track.

Texas Cocktails provides a snapshot of the state's drinking culture at a moment when craft cocktails are the rule, not the exception. This collection of recipes isn't exhaustive, because it can't be. Before you finish this paragraph, another solid bar will have opened in Dallas or Houston or El Paso. Another young bartender will have discovered the merits of a Daiquiri made with fresh juice or a well-balanced Negroni. The recipes, context, and bartender insights within aren't a compendium of everything Texas has to offer. They are representative of the evolving cocktail scene happening in the major cities and increasingly taking hold in every corner of this great state.

Enclosed, you won't find a detailed list of cocktail tools or a glossary of techniques and terms. By now, most drinkers understand the difference between a shaker and mixing glass, and it's easy enough to wield a strainer. Frankly, YouTube is a better medium for learning techniques. Consider this book your boozy tour of Texas—a fun-loving means of learning the people worth meeting and the places worth checking out. And know that if, by some Herculean effort, you're able to sample all of the featured cocktails, there will be many more just around the corner that are equally deserving of your attention.

It's an exciting time to be a drinker, not just in Texas but around the world. But as any Texan will quickly point out, everything here is just a little bigger and bolder. So, if there's something worth doing, whether it's mastering the classics or pushing boundaries in burgeoning categories, you can be damn sure it's happening somewhere within these borders.

Kevin Gray is a Dallas-based drinks writer and cofounder of Bevvy.

INTRODUCTION

★ ★ ★ ★ ★ ★ ★ ★ ★

INTRODUCTION

"IF A MAN'S FROM TEXAS, HE'LL TELL YOU.
IF HE'S NOT, WHY EMBARRASS HIM BY ASKING?"

- John Gunther

Texans are always in good spirits. This is home and we're happy to be here. Those who surround us are family and our family comes first. We're a prideful yet humble lot of straight shooters who are the friendliest people you'll ever meet. If you're in a bar in Texas, I promise you that you'll come out with more friends than you walked in with and you can hang your hat on it.

This book was originally a snapshot of Texas in 2017, but because of the nature of the service industry, since the original publication date, about one-quarter of the bars originally included have since closed. It's not entirely COVID-19's fault, but it certainly accelerated the process. By the time you read this, it will, again, be out of date, but the recipes will live forever. I can only hope that those who are mentioned and featured in this, in the last, and any future editions will continue to push this tall Texas tale into the future.

When Cider Mill Press asked me to write this book, the first thing I did was research all of the classic cocktails that came from Texas. I found both of them. I even cornered David Wondrich, the world's most celebrated cocktail historian, at a conference and asked him if I was missing anything. He told me about a commander at the battle of Sabine Pass who was also a saloon owner. (His name was Dick Dowling and his bar was Bank of Bacchus, one of the most popular places in in Houston in the 1860s.) There was a journal that mentioned the names of some of the drinks, but no recipes. He said, "I did a bunch of research on Texas a while back and that's all I ever found."

Frankly, the only two cocktails I could find that legitimately come from Texas are the Chilton and the Ranch Water… and we built the frozen margarita machine, for which we are sorry and not sorry. At this point in the process, I decided that I would let the best bars and bartenders represent our state and I'd do my best to get out of the way. Over a hundred cocktail recipes later, you have *Texas Cocktails.*

"Y'all know we're the size of Spain, right?" I told the publisher when we were discussing logistics. Texas is the epitome of vast. There are cocktail bars in LA that are closer to El Paso than McAllen and there are bars in Chicago that are closer to Texarkana than El Paso is. It's big here, y'all. That's why one of the key words to understanding Texas is diversity.

We're a little southern, a little western, a little Mexican, a little country, a little urban, a state with dramatic differences between our people, but a state that will fight tooth and nail for each other. We're American by birth and Texan by the grace of God. We've always been tough to categorize because we are our own category.

As for the cocktail scene, Texas has carved its own way. "There was nothing accidental about this," David Alan, author of *Tipsy Texan* and global brand ambassador for Patron told me. "It was not just right place, right time. It was active and it was a lot of work. It was things like if the newspaper wrote something inaccurate about bartenders, we'd write a letter to the newspaper. If a magazine wouldn't cover what you do correctly, we'd start writing for the magazine. If the distributors did carry something, we'd start calling. None of this was an accident." We worked for this. It was sheer Texan want-to that made this scene possible.

We're proud here. Texans are some of the most loyal and most prideful people you'll ever meet. We're also ridiculously friendly. For

Texans, we don't need to "get back to hospitality" as everyone else in the country seems to be screaming, we were born hospitable. The laid back, easy going, friendly, warm nature if Texans is exactly why we're good at this. This isn't a novelty. We don't have a cocktail or spirits tourism... yet. What we have are some of the most inventive bartenders rooted in friendliness. (Shout out to Bombay Sapphire's Most Imaginative Bartender, Justin Lavenue from Austin).

The Texas cocktail scene is world class in one respect: approachability. The bars that are thriving right now are neighborhood bars that happen to have stellar cocktail programs. We've moved beyond the nine-touch craziness, dialed everything back, and made it incredibly easy to get a proper cocktail here. Our cocktails are for anyone and everyone. Not only is it now impossible to open a restaurant without a cocktail menu of some sort, but the drinks on that menu have been specifically built to remove all intimidation. Even our most renowned bars were created to serve communities and not fads.

My great-grandfather came to Texas in a covered wagon from Morelos, Mexico. In fact, the area he stopped and set up shop had been Mexico less than eighty years prior. I've spent my entire life seeing the influence of Mexican culture on Texas and it didn't slow down when it came to cocktails. You'll never convince me that the place my great-grandfather hails from, you know, the place where the tequila, limes and agave come from, didn't invent the margarita, however, the margarita is, without question, the single most important drink in the state of Texas. The influence grows from there.

The staggering rise in popularity of tequila and mezcal? We might have had something to do with that. The idea of adding spice to cocktails? Hell, y'all's peppers aren't even hot. While the history of Texas spirits may start with Tito, we've been working with Mexican spirits since we were, well, Mexico.

We have the best grapefruit in the world. We have peaches that are rivaled only by Georgia. And look out Kentucky… but we're figuring out this whiskey thing pretty quickly. Just give us twelve more years to age it. I tried to honor the diversity of the state in the choices that were made for this book. I've tried to speak from my heart as a Texan and I've done my best to represent the state as a whole. The last thing I wanted to do was look at a map of where these cocktails came from and only see Dallas, Houston, Austin and San Antonio. The magical thing is that was possible. You can get a great margarita in Webster. Midland makes great Manhattans now. Denton and College Station, seminal Texas college towns, have great places to grab an old fashioned.

I asked David Alan what was different between when his book came out and now and he said, "Didn't you just tell me that you found one hundred and one different bars that serve proper cocktails? That's the difference." As Jeret Pena told me, we won. Cocktails have won. Now it becomes a battle to stand out in this scene… and not one Texan I know is afraid of a little competition.

Honorary Texan Jason Kosmas told me, "I think Texas is training more cocktail drinkers, by far, than any coast." Makes sense, doesn't it? So until you can visit these bars yourself, which is an experience that cannot be matched, I hand you these recipes. I hand you over a hundred recipes I, unapologetically, did not write. Most importantly, I hand you a small piece of the bigger story that I hope you will decide to join. But for now, I will let the geniuses in this state do what they're good at and I will get the hell out of the way.

HARVEYS FOR HARVEY

In August of 2017, when Hurricane Harvey hit Texas, it was one of the most terrifying and costly events the greater Houston area has ever seen. Entire communities under water, displaced people without homes, the smell of cut wood and mildew permeating the air... Can you genuinely imagine what it's like to be evacuated from your home as it is sinking into flood water, knowing that it's gone? Everything—every picture, every book, every favorite shirt, every teddy bear... gone. And at the time you're more interested in staying alive. And at the time you're trying to help your elderly neighbor. And at the time your adrenaline is so high that it never quite registers that you don't know if your insurance policy covers rising water.

At the time, you're too focused on saving others to realize that you've lost everything.

But you fight through, and the community around you rises up. The damage Harvey's inflicted cannot be undone, but the Gulf Coast community in Texas has united to help their brothers and sisters get through this. The same can be said for the service industry.

The Harvey Wallbanger is one of the most incredible initiatives I've ever seen. Over $250,000 was raised by bars and bartenders across the world to benefit the victims of Hurricane Harvey. Over 500 bars participated by doing what they do best... selling cocktails.

The Harvey Wallbanger is a simple drink that will now live in infamy. This is, in fact, a recipe book, so I thought I'd include it.

When Harveys for Harvey became a rallying cry, Lucas Bols, makers of Galliano, stepped up in a huge way. They donated all profits from the sales of Galliano in September to relief efforts in the greater Houston area. On top of that, they helped with publicity and coordination and they never asked for anything in return. I'm not writing this because I got a press release about it, I'm writing this because they made a difference.

Other brands matched donations or contributed products to fundraisers all over the state and the nation. The United States Bartenders' Guild San Antonio Chapter raised $15,000, and the Dallas

Chapter raised over $40,000. There are thousands of members of "Service Industry for Harvey Relief" groups on Facebook and events are still happening.

The resiliency of the Houston service industry is a true inspiration, and the impact of these industry fundraisers is quite real. Bobby Heugel said it best: "Thank you to everyone that donated to help our city, bought a Harvey Wallbanger, or just did something for people anywhere in need this last month and a half. When you watch an event like this happen first-hand, you realize how small and helpless you are as an individual. And then, when you watch everyone band together and respond, humanity's real strength becomes apparent. There are currently and will be more challenges ahead—there always are. Our only real option for overcoming them is together."

HARVEY WALLBANGER

The Harvey Wallbanger was, more than likely, the creation of a marketing team in the late 1960s. By 1969, the character "Harvey Wallbanger" appeared in everything from pop art to bumper stickers. This silly little cocktail began to appear on reputable cocktail menus again in the early 2000s after Galliano switched back to their original recipe.

Glassware: **Tall Glass**

- **1.25 oz vodka**
- **3 oz orange juice**
- **.5 oz Galliano L'Autentico**

1. Combine orange juice and vodka in a tall glass with ice.

2. Stir and float Galliano on top.

3. Garnish with an orange slice.

DRINK LIKE A TEXAN

How do you drink like a Texan? Grab a fajita and let's do this...

★ Your pregame is Topo Chico or Dr. Pepper. Or probably Shiner.

★ When you toast, you tap the table before you drink. Cheers to the future but acknowledge the past.

★ If it's a celebration, you're raising a glass. If it's a tailgate or it's a baptism, odds are there's a keg... and a surly uncle with a handle of whiskey.

★ Beer is the King, but Margarita is our Queen.

★ Cowboy boots are for every occasion. Whether you're at a black-tie gala or literally roping a calf, boots are the footwear of choice.

★ We like hot sauce on our hot sauce.

★ Our first drink was either a frozen margarita given to us as a tiny sip by our favorite aunt at a hole-in-the-wall Mexican joint, or a sip of beer at a family reunion, probably given to us by the same surly uncle who brought the handle of whiskey.

★ Our hospitality is as Southern as it gets.

★ If you're floating the river, your best raft holds the beer.

★ If you want to sneak booze into a football game, you put a flask in your boot. Everybody knows that.

★ Check your degree at the door. We don't care if you're a doctor or a ranch hand, no one pulls rank inside the bar.

TEXAS COCKTAILS SOUNDTRACK

Music is done a little differently in Texas. From the roots of outlaw country to some of the best hip hop in the nation, Texas music is as diverse as it's cocktails. I asked my friend Mark Schectman to help design the perfect soundtrack to cruise around to these great cocktail spots. He hosts a weekly new music radio show called 'The Local Ticket' that can be heard every Sunday night on Sportsradio 1310/96.7FM The Ticket in Dallas. He's the creator of #fancydranks and the proud owner of a super-secret speakeasy called The Hitchcock, which can only be accessed through his side yard. Mark once told me, "I like cocktails because they make me feel fancy." You and me both, pal.

Old 97's - Niteclub

An ode to the special relationship you have with your favorite bar...and the people that frequent that bar.

Ben Kweller - Wasted and Ready

We're not saying you shouldn't imbibe responsibly. We're also not saying that we've never felt this feeling before.

The Texas Gentlemen - Habbie Doobie

A raucous 6:17 exploration of Americana, honky tonk and good times.

St. Vincent - What, Me Worry?

There's nothing like a sweet song wrapped in an Arrested Development reference that sounds like a French 75 tastes.

Beyonce - 7/11

Pairs well with the "Hot Mess" from Vox Table in Austin (page 150) and the "What Really Happened" from Houston Watch Company (page 98).

Blue the Misfit - Child of the Night

Day drinking is fun and all, but some of us just hit another gear after the sun goes down.

Ghostland Observatory - Life of the Party

Shout out to the heroes that help the host clean up.

Son of Stan - Loseyomind

The king of divorce pop makes you wanna dance. Pairs well with awkward bar conversations and whiskey.

Charlie Crockett - Just a Drink Away

Dallas bluesman channels the memory of Ernest Tubb's tune about good ol' fashioned heartache.

White Denim - Corsicana Lemonade
Austin psychedelic prog-rock dabbling taking you on a tour of Texas with a lemonade in hand.

T-Bird and The Breaks - Blackberry Brandy
A little extra money, or a delicious drink? If only all choices in life could be this easy.

The Reverend Horton Heat - Please Don't Take the Baby to the Liquor Store
Don't tell me what to do, Rev. We've done this. You should too.

Lyle Lovett - That's Right (You're Not From Texas)
A tune about Southern (Texan) hospitality. Even if you're not from Texas, we're glad you're here.

Pat Green - Take Me Out to a Dance Hall
Ahh alcohol...As the philosopher Homer J. Simpson once said, it's the cause of and solution to all of life's problems.

Waylon Jennings - Sunday Morning Coming Down
Don't think of it as a hangover. Think of it as a night well spent.

—Show de Vie—

I like to think of Mike G as the documentarian that we don't deserve. His podcast is well over the 200-episode threshold and he's not slowing down at all. If you have any desire to completely nerd out on all things cocktail, subscribe to *Show de Vie*. It's practically a grad school education through an audio medium. Mike is capturing all of the stories that would disappear without him and bless him for it. I had a chance to turn the tables and do a quick interview with him having to answer the questions.

When (and how) did you start *Show de Vie?*

After a meal with a family friend in September 2015, I was regaled with these incredible stories about Hollywood and the booze industry. The gentleman had few living relatives and a son who he was at odds with. If these stories went undocumented or captured, it'd be a loss to the industry as a whole. I got the mics out of retirement and started capturing as much as possible.

Why did you decide to document this scene in this manner, and why is documentation important?

Most of our knowledge of the key personalities in this industry is through the lens of a brand. But what if instead of brand forward dialogues, we had people-focused narratives? The journeys of others are a great predictor and template for learning about our own paths. No more important resurgence of cocktail culture will occur this century, so now it's essential to capture the essence and vibrancy of the scene. It's imperative to document this era in an unfettered, unrestrained, and unfiltered way. I hope these chats serve as some kind of reference material for a great period in hospitality.

How has the Texas cocktail scene changed in the last 10 years?

All about that fresh juice. The connection to raw materials and raw ingredients in the culinary scene has been the impetus for a shift in cocktail culture in Texas. When you couple a keen curiosity about terroir, construction, and production with technology, the modern era of cocktails is all about intellectual empowerment. Both creativity and careers behind the bar are being rewarded and acknowledged as legitimate endeavors now. They are lucrative jobs that now assert their place at the forefront of consumer minds in Texas. Texas went from slinging Jack and Cokes to preparing a freshly squeezed margarita. Once the efforts were recognized by the media and general public, more and more people started feeling comfortable with adventurous cocktails. The past ten years have been the age of enlightenment with regard to food and drinks. Manhattans are a household name now.

What makes a cocktail uniquely Texan?

I think more than any other "genre" of cocktail, Texans love to add heat to their cocktails. Our acclimation to the Southwest cuisine and agave spirits make them a conscious influence on how we create. Hot summers, ubiquitous tequila—these create the perfect backdrop for heat, acidity, and a boozy punch. We're able to deal with huge levels of heat, frustration, and a massive population in Texas. We need a drink that pays homage to our unique culture and tenacity. Make it spicy and strong, we can handle it.

What immediately comes to mind when I say the phrase "Texas Cocktails"?

The outdoors. Ingredients with some rusticity. Hearty and strong willed.

WINE
BEER

PROHIBITION IN TEXAS

In the years leading up to Prohibition, Texas was becoming drier and drier. There was a very active Temperance movement in Texas, and they quickly gained support in rural areas, while the cities and the borderlands continued to be free-flowing. Eight months before the Volstead Act was signed, Texas entered into their own prohibition. In fact, Senator Morris Sheppard, from Morris County, is known as the "Father of National Prohibition," for writing the 18th Amendment. For that, we're sorry… Sidenote, during Prohibition, a still that produced 130 gallons of moonshine per day was discovered on a ranch in Texas that Sheppard owned. No wonder it was repealed fourteen years later… even the "Father of National Prohibition" didn't really mean it.

In Houston in 1927, a 600-gallon still was seized from a seven-room house built to look like a farmhouse-style shack, similar to the other small houses off Westheimer Road. The house was built for moonshining, but the windows were staged with lace curtains and fake headboards. There was a known cluster of Italian immigrants who operated a series of moonshine stills in the area. According to the *Post-Dispatch,* "246 gallons of whisky valued at $2,000 was found in one of the rooms stored in charred cypress and oak casks. A 600-gallon copper still was seized and destroyed by the officers. Other equipment included a 300-gallon cooling tank, pumps that lifted the mash from the barrels to the still, pipes that carried the refuse into a nearby cotton field and some mixing equipment." I'm secretly hoping this happened where Poison Girl is now and they find a barrel of whiskey from 1927 during the next renovation.

In Galveston, it was rum running and open era time. The period is sometimes referred to as the *open era* or the *wide-open era,* because the community made extremely little effort to hide the illegal vices. A rum row, with boats from Cuba, Jamaica, and the Bahamas, was

established 35 miles of the coast. Small boats would fetch the goods and bring them back to the Galveston shore. This was so profitable that some of the most famous rum runners, Rose and Sam Maceo, were able to open Hollywood Dinner Club, which was the most sophisticated night club on the Gulf Coast. During Prohibition the Maceos were able to gain control of Galveston's underground society, where they ran casinos, speakeasies, and night clubs. Their most famous, the Balinese Room, opened in 1929. (Be sure to check out the cocktail with the same name from Lei Low in Houston.) Not even the Great Depression was slowing Galveston down, and at one point the Maceos owned as many as sixty clubs with slot machines.

In El Paso, the border became a draw for tourists from across the United States, including politicians. In fact, in the 1920s the El Paso Chamber of Commerce found ways to promote their "Tour of Mexico," which was basically a drinking tour. Built to serve the vice

habits of Americans, Juarez boomed. A number of American distillers moved to Juarez to set up shop. Mary Dowling hired Joseph L. Beam, who was considered the best distiller in Kentucky and was suddenly out of work, to disassemble the entire Waterfill & Frazier Distillery in Kentucky and then reassemble it in Juarez, Mexico, in order to resume legal production of whiskey. Once Joseph left Juarez three years later, he went on to found a little company called Heaven Hill.

The biggest impact Prohibition had on the United States was the disappearance of spirits history. Prohibition was just long enough to destroy smaller distillers who couldn't wait for this terrible social experiment to end. It destroyed the craft. And when it was repealed, only the big guys were still standing. This led to decade upon decade of limited American spirit options. After Prohibition, it was sixty-three years before there was a legal distillery in Texas.

MAKERS VS. FAKERS

By Mark McDavid,
Ranger Creek Brewing & Distilling

Craft distilling is exploding in the United States, which is resulting in more and more new products on the shelves at your favorite liquor stores. Some of these products are exciting, authentic, and delicious. However, if you take notice and look more closely, many of these products are inauthentic in their claims and sold under false pretenses. What you might think is a local, craft-distilled whiskey might actually be mass produced by a large industrial factory in Indiana.

This misrepresentation is happening in Texas right now. While you might see over a dozen products labeled as "Texas Whiskey" on the shelf, only a small number are actually made in Texas.

So how do you tell the makers from the fakers? When you see a spirit labeled as "Texas Whiskey," how do you know if it was actually made in Texas or sourced from out of state? While there's still not one easy answer, following these guidelines will make you an educated shopper. While Ranger Creek makes all of our Texas whiskey, we don't believe that sourcing whiskey from another company is inherently bad. The problem comes with misrepresenting sourced whiskey as hand-crafted and local. Use these guidelines to tell the difference.

1. The Label

The label is your best source for truth. Spirits labels have to be approved through the Alcohol and Tobacco Tax and Trade Bureau (TTB), a federal agency that oversees the certificates of label approval required for all spirits prior to interstate commerce. Since a federal regulator scrutinizes every word on a whiskey label, the verbiage on the label really matters. Look for the words "Distilled by." Usually it's in small print on the back. "Distilled by" means that the company actually distilled the product. If you see the words "Produced by," "Manufactured by," "Bottled by," "Filled by," "Blended by", or any others, those are red flags. The only term approved by the TTB for those that actually make their stuff is "Distilled." Although the label is your best resource, companies and regulators do sometimes make mistakes, so it's not fool proof. Look for the below phrases on a label to spot a faker or maker.

Fakers

"Bottled by" is a red flag.

"Produced and bottled" is NOT "distilled," even if it was done with care.

"Blended and bottled" means alcohol is purchased from others. Note: Go Texan logo can be used on inauthentic Texas whiskeys.

Makers

"Distilled and bottled by" means they made it.

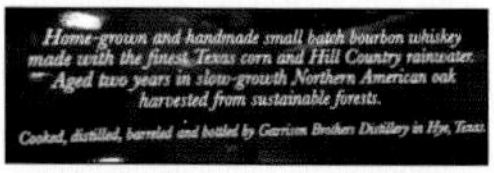

"Cooked, distilled, barreled, and bottled." No doubt that this is authentic.

"Fermented, distilled, matured, and bottled." Also no doubt that this is actually made in Texas.

2. The Timeline

If a 1–2 year old distillery is putting out a 5–6 year old whiskey, that's a HUGE red flag. It's also really common. Any new distillery that automatically has really old whiskey on the market has to be sourcing it. If you have a question, do some digging on the company's website to find out when they started distilling.

3. The Price Point

If you see a typical 750 ml bottle of Texas whiskey for $25, it's sourced. Craft distilleries are almost all new, which means we're still small. We also typically use premium ingredients and do almost everything by hand. For instance, all of the corn we use in our Texas bourbon is Texas corn. Texas corn is typically more expensive than non-Texas corn, but we're committed to using local ingredients. The economics of making craft whiskey means our stuff is generally more expensive.

Here's an example of a distillery that offers a product they distilled and one they purchased:

Guess which one is not made there and which one is authentic:

"Produced and bottled" is around $30.

"Distilled and bottled" is around $50.

4. Liquor Store Employees

Although we have met many liquor store employees who are passionate about truth in Texas whiskey, there are often corporate policies that prevent them from communicating it to consumers. Some inauthentic whiskey brands have agreements with liquor chains that compensate them for each bottle sold. Those agreements turn into policies that require employees to push certain brands. So if you ask an average employee which Texas whiskey they recommend, you won't know if they're recommending it on their own accord or because of corporate policy.

5. Distillery Websites

Distillery websites and other marketing collateral are probably the worst resources for determining makers and fakers. None of this material is scrutinized through the government like labels are, so there is a lot of room for obfuscation. Fakers use images of stills and aging barrels to confuse you. Unless you read and analyze each word like a lawyer, it is very difficult to determine if they are a maker or a faker. We believe in transparency, but there is not very much of that going on right now. A few distilleries that sell sourced brands are honest about it, and whiskey drinkers commend them for their transparency.

6. Other Indicators for Makers

Many makers of true craft whiskey use unusual ingredients like oat, millet, quinoa, or, in our case, mesquite-smoked malt. The industrial manufacturers don't use these ingredients, so that's a good sign of a maker. Makers also typically brag about the fact that their whiskey is truly made from grain to glass and will brag about every step of the process being done at their distillery.

MEZCAL IN TEXAS

Emma Janzen, author of *Mezcal: The History, Craft & Cocktails of the World's Ultimate Artisanal Spirit*

You don't have to look much further than the ubiquitous margarita for proof that Texas has long held a deep appreciation for Mexican spirits. Tequila particularly has always had a home at the bar in the Lone Star State, so perhaps it's no surprise that Texans also quickly stepped up as early advocates for mezcal—the predecessor of tequila and godfather of Mexican spirits that

is made from various species of the agave plant—when the category started its dramatic ascent in America.

Until brands like Del Maguey, Ilegal, Sombra, and Fidencio started trickling over the border, most mezcal available in the US was of poor quality, and its reputation reflected the scorpion-laden swill in the bottle. With its inherently smoky qualities and higher-than-average proof, mezcal was considered the drunkard's choice for so long that the category didn't see much attention until pioneers like Ron Cooper and others began spreading the gospel of Mexico's most soulful spirit.

In Texas specifically, bartenders quickly realized mezcal's diverse range of flavor and mixing potential. Early adopters started stocking back bars in places like La Condesa and Takoba in Austin, Esquire

Tavern and Ocho Lounge in San Antonio, Bolsa in Dallas, and The Pastry War in Houston with better quality bottles by the case-full. In these places, where bartenders like Bobby Heugel, Alba Huerta, Jeret Peña, Eddie "Lucky" Campbell, Bill Norris, and others were creating thoughtful agave-centric menus, the spirit also naturally found a home in cocktails—one of the best introductions to the smoky, mysterious liquid for the uninitiated. Some have risen to the status of Texas icons, like Heugel's bold and unwavering The Brave from Anvil Bar & Refuge and Eaves' Texecutioner from Esquire Tavern.

Now, Texas plays home to many full-blown mezcaleria-style bars with selections that dwarf those in many other locales, like Mezcaleria Tobala and Techo in Austin, Captain Foxheart's Bad News Bar in Houston, and Dallas' Las Almas Rotas. Creative cocktails abound, and more people than ever are becoming familiar with the virtues of sip-

ping mezcal neat (with some sal de gusano on the side, of course). As long as new school brands like Mezcal Vago, El Jolgorio, Rey Campero, Real Minero, and Don Mateo continue to bring exceptional mezcal to Texas, you can be sure agave lovers will keep the momentum going strong.

TECHNOLOGY IN THE BAR

By Scott Jenkins, HIDE Bar

Innovation within the bar industry is nothing new. Bartenders tend to naturally evolve by learning and mastering classic recipes, riffing off those, and then moving on to their own concoctions. I would think it's safe to say, as it was in my case, most will make a lot of crap cocktails before they make good ones. Making great cocktails requires a few things in my opinion: curiosity and willingness to take risk; an ever-developing palette; a sensitivity and understanding of the materials you are working with; a program which provides the freedom to explore; accuracy; and a solid system for ego-checking.

I would never claim that this is the only way to approach cocktails. It is however, my preferred method. I firmly believe that cocktails (I would include food in this as well) are a language. The spirits we use have a specific history and design, an accent if you will, that gives them a certain character profile of expression. These things may seem pretentious to some, but I believe that these spirits produce a syntax used in the formation story a cocktail can tell, the story of right now. The structure of the experience one has with the cocktail right in front of them, and the perceptions which can be distinguished, give us insight into how aware of the moment we are: presentation, color, body, texture, acidity, top notes, middle notes, finishing notes, acidity, sweetness, intensity, salinity, etc. Why is this important? Because it is a direct reminder that you are alive and experiencing something. For me, this is electric and one of the reasons I am so particular about how I design and serve my cocktails.

Why Use Technology in the Bar?

Why not? Costs aside for a moment, why would you not use tools to help your craft excel? We all use bar tools, and we prefer them based off our own methodology; One can think of these as the next level extension of that tool kit. My first piece of advice for you, if you are considering using the tech below, is to not be a dick about it. NO ONE will care about your fancy equipment if you're shoving it in everyone's face as some sort of gimmick. Dispense with the theatricality that has crept its way into the scene and just put your head down and do the work. The tech is designed to allow for specific things to happen within your program, and should be left to functionality. That isn't to say that the process you used shouldn't be talked about or explained to your patrons. If they show an interest, then by all means nerd out!

Centrifuge

This is a workhorse in my program. It allows us to do many things ranging from juice clarification to blending spirits with fruit, which aids in extracting flavor without keeping the particulate from the fruit. You can purchase large units, that are refrigerated, and spin 3–4 liters of liquid at about 5000 rpm. Or, thanks to Dave Arnold of Booker and Dax, you can purchase a tabletop centrifuge which does everything a large unit can do with a different operation style. There are many resources for why these techniques are great, and you should check them out.

Rotary-Evaporator

This machine is expensive and temperamental, but cool to use. Essentially, this is a flavor scalpel, meaning you can add or strip away flavors from spirits if you know what you're doing. We use this to infuse spirits with different flavors such as habanero (the capsaicin that delivers the heat doesn't transfer), cilantro, and delicate flavors such as rose petal or chamomile. You can produce spirits that have flavors infused at the molecular level as opposed to letting product soak in the spirits for a few days. This allows for greater control over flavor expression in cocktails, and allows the product to be kept indefinitely without spoilage from oxidation or molding of leftover particulates. This rig can also be used to create essential oils, infused bitters, concentrated syrups, and hydrosols.

Carbonation

We have a system at HIDE which allows us to carbonate cocktails with tiny champagne-sized bubbles in a controlled manner. This creates a clean and crisp texture to anything we carbonate, and we test-carbonate everything we can, just because we can. If you're interested in creating your own sparkling cocktails, or sodas, take heed with this tech and research the science behind it, because carbonation is an art form.

These are just a few techniques we use at HIDE to create the most balanced, delicious, and flavorful cocktails we can dream up. There are many more techniques, machinery, and ingredients we utilize in our program, but the aforementioned should give anyone a good start at creating some truly unique experiences for their guests.

WHERE TO BUY

The Austin Shaker
1199 Airport Blvd, Austin, TX 78702

When Kiki and David came to Austin from Boston, they noticed there wasn't a place they could get the "weird stuff"... combine that with a liquor store coming up for sale around the corner from their house, and the Austin Shaker was born. This is where Austin keeps their spirits weird. If they have distribution, and they're cool, odds are you'll find it here.

Bar & Garden
3314 Ross Ave, Ste 150, Dallas, TX 75204

While they originally started in LA, there's only one other location, and that's in Dallas. Bar & Garden is exceedingly cool. With their mission to only sell all-natural wines and then spirits as well, Bar and Garden is like a cheat sheet for knowing who the highest quality producers are.

Tricks of the Trade - *Spirits and Supplies*
219 S Main Street, Fort Worth, TX 76104

After spending years as the best bartender in Fort Worth, Megan McClinton decided to open up her own bottle shop to support the growing cocktail scene in Fort Worth. This is where the good stuff is.

Houston Wine Merchant
2646 S Shepherd Dr, Houston, TX 77098

Don't let the name fool you… Houston Wine Merchant has one of the best specialty spirits selections in Houston. With tasting every Friday and Saturday, they've been a catalyst in the education of the Houstonian for more than 30 years.

Pig Liquors
519 S Presa St, San Antonio, TX 78205

If they don't have it, you ain't getting it. Southtown's best is also San Antonio's. Anet Alaniz owns the best specialty liquor spot in San Antonio, and she's always helping her clients source anything she might not have in stock. This funky spot will make you smile.

Twin Liquors
Locations across Texas

Twin Liquors is probably the best of the best chain liquor stores. They're consistently knowledgeable and the selection is incredible. Born in Austin and now across the state, Twin Liquors has been a part of the Texas spirits scene for over 80 years.

TEXAS BORN, TEXAS MADE

1888 Dirtiest Martini Mix

When Kenneth Hamburger wanted his martini dirtier and dirtier, he became obsessed with the way that olive juice was being used in cocktails. He decided to create an olive juice that's closer to wine than the liquid where most olives live. He uses a one-ton press to extract the juice from whole Spanish olives, and it gives you a true olive flavor with no aftertaste. If you're into dirty martinis, this is your new best friend.

Andalusia Whiskey Company

Ty Phelps and Tommy Erwin, formerly of Real Ale Brewing Company, have focused their distillery on three whiskeys: the Revenant Oak, which is a peated single malt, the White Pearl, which is their white whiskey; and the Stryker, which is a smoked single malt. As these puppies age, I think they're going to start garnering national recognition. Watch out for these dudes.

Bloody Revolution

Genuinely, some of the best Bloody Mary mixers I've had come from Austin. Longtime friends Chantz Hoover and Greg Bodle decided that their favorite drink, the Bloody Mary, deserved as much of a craft treatment as the rest of the cocktails out there, and they made Bloody Revolution. With six flavors, each provides a different, but delicious, way to approach your favorite brunch cocktail. And the Ribeye flavor is basically steak in a glass, which doesn't suck in the slightest.

Elk Store Winery & Distillery

Czech brothers Todd Smajstrla and Scott Hladky are carrying on their family tradition of moonshining at this Fredricksburg distillery. And yes, the majority of great-grand-daddy's moonshining did come during Prohibition. You'll have to visit Elk Store to try their selection of spirits including pecan pie moonshine, oak-infused moonshine, white rum, and old tom gin, to name a few. They are not distributed, but if you find yourself in wine country, go have yourself a moonshine.

Martine Honeysuckle Liqueur

I remember as a kid being at my abuelita's house smelling, picking, and sucking the nectar out of honeysuckle right off the plant. Honeysuckle plays a role in almost every Texan's childhood at some point. Gary Kelleher, the co-founder of Dripping Springs Vodka, spent five years perfecting his honeysuckle liqueur recipe. Kelleher wanted Martine to not only taste like a honeysuckle in blossom, but to also capture the aroma of the flower. Martine does both, beautifully.

Monjus Spirits

The Monju story involves a 19th century move from the Balearic Islands in Spain to New Orleans, continues with a distilling operation on Burgundy Street in the French Quarter, and begins again with finding an ancient family recipe book. Monju is just starting, but they're one of the products I'm most looking forward to. They make several varieties of Spanish-grape-based absinthes and are definitely one to watch.

Marfa Spirits

Launched in 2019, the team at Marfa has been working closely with sotol producers in Chihuahua, Mexico to ensure their Texas version of the traditionally Mexican spirit will pay homage to its ancestors. Located in a 1920s-era grain mill in the heart of Marfa, this is one of the most up and coming distilleries in the state.

Paula's Texas Spirits

Paula Angerstein received the second distiller's license in Texas, after Tito, in 2003 and launched Paula's Texas Orange and Paula's Texas Lemon. Her flavors are based on more of a limoncello style than typical orange liqueurs and are usually around twice the proof. Paula was one of the first female distillers in the United States, and her products can be found in bars and on menus arcoss the state.

Railean American Made Rum

Railean started in 2005 when Kelly Railean quit her corporate job and started to champion the very spirit that fueled the American revolution. Located in San Leon, on the shores of Galveston Bay with all of the history of rum running in that part of the world, it seem appropriate that Railean was the first woman-owned distillery to make American rum.

Grayson Blended Texas Bourbon

Full disclosure... since the original publishing of this book, I've made a whiskey. Batch 1 of Grayson is a blend of Ironroot, Balcones, and Lone Elm distilleries and you'll just have to stay tuned to see who's involved in future batches.

CLASSIC Cocktails

★★★★★★★★★★★★★★★★★★★★★★★★★★★★★

"YOU MAY ALL GO TO HELL AND I WILL GO TO TEXAS."

—Davy Crockett

We don't have a lot of classic cocktail history that originated from the Lone Star State. In fact, the two "classics" that absolutely came from here are both pretty micro regional in nature, but both quite popular across Texas today. Now, if you order them in Denver on the other hand, you may get a blank stare. However, there are plenty of quintessential Texas drinks that have formed the cocktail culture as we know it. Margaritas, Palomas, even the dreaded and feared Mexican Martini, have all provided the foundation of the Texas cocktail movement, and for that reason, you better know how to make a frozen margarita.

★★★★★★★★★★★★★★★★★★★★★★★★★★★★★

CHILTON

The Chilton is one of the two "classic" cocktails that can be attributed to Texas. According to members of the Lubbock Country Club, a local doctor, Dr. Chilton to be exact, asked his bartender to mix the juice of two lemons with vodka and soda and serve it over ice, with a salt rim. Ta-dah! Chilton! It's a sunny and dry panhandle day in a glass. That's one thing about these West Texas cocktails... they're always as dry as the land they come from.

Glassware: **Highball Glass**
Garnish: **Lemon Wheel**

- **1.5 oz Texas vodka (try Dripping Springs or Cinco)**
- **Juice of 2 lemons**
- **Topo Chico**

1. Rim a highball glass with salt, then fill it with ice.

2. Add vodka and lemon juice, then top with Topo Chico and stir.

3. Garnish with a lemon wheel.

FROZEN MARGARITA

In Dallas in 1971, Mariano Martinez had a problem. Too many people wanted margaritas and it was taking too long to make them. After a sleepless night, Mariano stopped by a convenience store on the way to work for coffee, saw a slushie machine, and the rest is history. Soon, he was making margaritas in a soft-serve ice-cream machine, and he called it "The World's First Frozen Margarita Machine." Over time, the frozen margarita has undoubtedly become the most popular cocktail in the entire state of Texas. When I sat down with Bobby Heugel, I asked which cocktail was the quintessential Texas cocktail and he responded, "A frozen margarita. They serve them at every tex-mex place in the state and it's the drink that we were given sips of as kids. It's the frozen margarita, definitely."

Glassware: **Margarita Glass or Frozen Mug**
Garnish: **Lime Wedge**

- **2 oz blanco tequila**
- **1 oz fresh lime juice**
- **.75 oz Cointreau**

1. Add tequila, lime juice and Cointreau along with 1 cup of ice to your blender. Blend until smooth.

2. Pour into a chilled, salted margarita glass or frozen mug.

3. Garnish with a lime wheel.

David Alan (*Tipsy Texan*) believes that "the drink is essentially a margarita presented in a cocktail shaker and then poured tableside into a cocktail glass rimmed with salt and garnished with a jalapeño-stuffed olive. At its worst it is shaken with Rose's lime juice or other adulterants." I completely agree. So if I was to try to make my own Mexican Martini, this is the recipe I'd go with.

MEXICAN MARTINI

Oh the Mexican Martini … so popular in Texas, yet so bizarre. I felt the need to include this based solely on its meteoric rise in popularity in Texas (specifically Austin) and the fact that, odds are, someone behind the bar will be able to make it. There's debate as to where the drink originated and which approach is best, but I will say that if you're going to wade into the waters of the Mexican Martini, leave the Sprite and orange juice at home. This is two drinks, and two strong ones at that. Consume only on a patio with chips, salsa, queso, and guacamole on the table, preferably while waiting for the fajitas to finish grilling.

Glassware: **Martini Glass**
Garnish: **Jalapeño-Stuffed Olive**

- **3 oz reposado tequila**
- **1.5 oz Cointreau**
- **1.5 oz fresh lime juice**
- **.5 oz 1888 Dirtiest Martini Mix**

1. Combine ingredients in a shaker with ice and shake vigorously.

2. Strain into a chilled martini glass, rimmed with salt.

3. Leave remaining cocktail in the shaker and refill glass as needed.

PALOMA

The history of this drink is unclear; however, credit is usually given to Don Javier Delgado Corona from the La Capilla bar in Jalisco, Mexico, and it's said that he might have named it after a folk song from the 1860s called "La Paloma." Margaritas have taken over the United States, but in Mexico, where the tequila comes from, it's the Paloma. The first case in print is rumored to be by Evan Harrison who wrote *Popular Cocktails of The Rio Grande.* Traditionally, this cocktail includes grapefruit soda, like Jarritos, but I prefer it with fresh grapefruit and Topo Chico. I mean, when you have some of the best in the world, why would you not?

Glassware: **Collins Glass**
Garnish: **Grapefruit slice**

- **1 oz fresh grapefruit juice**
- **.5 oz fresh lime juice**
- **.5 oz agave nectar**
- **1.5 oz blanco tequila**
- **Topo Chico**

1. Combine ingredients, except Topo Chico, in a shaker with ice and shake vigorously.

2. Strain into a collins glass with ice. Top with Topo Chico.

3. Garnish with a grapefruit slice.

RANCH WATER

When the first version of this book was published in 2018, the Ranch Water was a little-known cocktail with an adorable cult following. Since then, it has exploded. This is THE Texas cocktail that will forever be associated with our state. This is, absolutely, the most important of all Texas cocktails. Nowadays, there are as many versions of the cocktails origin as there are cans claiming to be "Ranch Water" being sold at Bucee's. But don't buy any of that garbage. You're better than that.

This uniquely West Texas drink is rumored to have started in the 1960s. The Gage Hotel in Marathon, after years of making the drink for those requesting it, made it official by putting the drink on the menu in 2010. It's also rumored to have started in Austin in the 90's, so who the hell knows... What we are sure of, is that Ranch Water is the epitome of simplicity, and you can sip on them all day. Plenty of bars across the US have tried to fancy or sweeten up the Ranch Water by adding simple syrup or clarifying lime juice or even swapping the tequila for different spirits, but those aren't Ranch Waters. Don't buy any of that garbage. You're better than that.

Glassware: **Topo Chico**
Garnish: **Lime Wedge**

- **12 oz bottle of Topo Chico**
- **1.5 oz blanco tequila**
- **.25 oz fresh lime juice**

1. Start by pouring out two ounces of the Topo Chico.

2. Add the tequila and lime juice to the Topo Chico bottle.

3. Garnish with lime wedge.

TEXAS FIZZ

The Texas Fizz ain't from Texas y'all. Two London-based bartenders first published this cocktail recipe in 1922, smack dab in the middle of Prohibition, meaning the citizens of this cocktail's namesake couldn't even have one! Originally the recipe called for seltzer, but in 1936 Frank Meier of the Ritz Hotel in Paris published a recipe replacing the seltzer with champagne to kick it up a notch. And rightfully so… I mean, if you're going to use our name, it needs to be a little more interesting than gin, juice, and seltzer.

Glassware: **Collins Glass**
Garnish: **Orange Twist**

- **1.5 oz London dry gin**
- **.5 oz fresh lemon juice**
- **.75 oz fresh orange juice**
- **.25 oz grenadine**
- **2–3 oz chilled brut champagne**

1. Combine ingredients in a shaker with ice and shake vigorously.

2. Strain into a chilled collins glass and top with champagne.

TOMMY'S MARGARITA

If you're going to do a margarita, do Tommy's Margarita bypass the orange liqueur and hit it with agave. This version of the margarita was created by Julio Bermejo at Tommy's Mexican Restaurant in San Francisco in the 1990s. This is simply the freshest approach to a simple margarita. Memorize this one.

Glassware: **Margarita Glass**
Garnish: **Salt, for rimming (optional), and Lime Wedge**

- **2 oz tequila, 100% agave**
- **1 oz lime juice**
- **.5 oz agave nectar**

1. Combine ingredients in a shaker with ice and shake vigorously.

2. Strain into a margarita glass, rimmed with salt.

3. Garnish with lime wedge.

CHAIRMAN'S
RESERVE
RUM
MEZCALOSFERA
Rhum J.M
Rhum J.M
V.O
EL DORADO
12

CREATIVE Concoctions

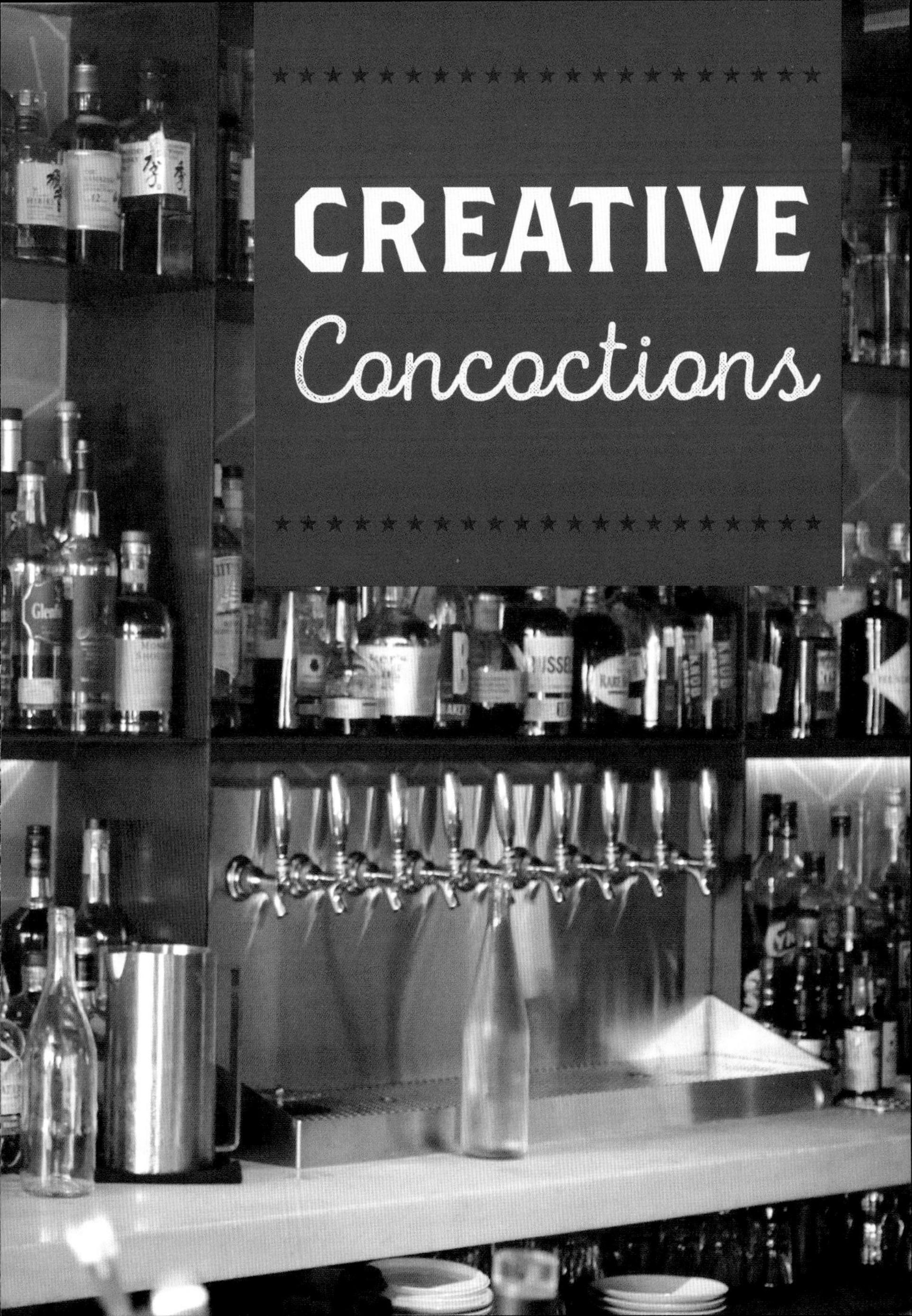

"IF YOU'RE JUST GOING TO DO WHAT EVERYBODY ELSE HAS DONE BEFORE, WHO CARES?"

—Chip Tate

When you go to a bar like The Aviary in Chicago or Dandelyan in London, you'll see some of the most imaginative uses of technology in the cocktail world but because of the way that information spreads nowadays, these ideas are migrating.

In Texas, while we're certainly laidback in our approach to most of life, we can execute a cocktail with the expertise and precision of the best bartenders in the world. This chapter has a few examples of some of the inventive approaches you can find in this rapidly advancing cocktail community. These are cocktails that you should absolutely try to make at home... if you have all of the stuff to do so and don't mind diving down the rabbit hole a bit.

LANDRACE

Esquire Tavern Downstairs
Recipe: Myles Worrell, Downstairs, 2016
155 E Commerce St
San Antonio, TX 78205
(210) 222-2521
esquiretavern-sa.com/downstairs

Okay, so … here's a little secret … there's a speakeasy inside a cocktail bar in San Antonio. Meta, I know. But the Downstairs at Esquire Tavern is truly a different world from the raucous party happening above. With Hank Cathey coming up with some of the most innovative drinks and drink presentations in the city, Downstairs is an experience in and of its own. With an entrance on the Riverwalk itself, Downstairs is an intimate lounge dishing out "unconventional inclinations." This place is nice. I'm talking really nice. This isn't a cocktail dive bar… this is, unquestionably, the nicest bar on the Riverwalk and the drinks are absolutely incredible.

Glassware: **Cocktail Glass**
Garnish: **Orange Twist**

- **2 oz Blue Corn gin**
- **1 oz Huitlachoche vermouth**
- **1 oz Luxardo maraschino liqueur**
- **1 dash Regan's orange bitters**
- **1 dash Bittermens Scarborough bitters**

1. Stir all ingredients well with ice in a mixing glass, and strain into a chilled cocktail glass.

2. Express oil from a large swath of orange peel over the drink, and garnish with an orange twist.

Blue Corn Gin

- 8 oz landrace Mexican blue corn
- 1L Greenall's gin

Combine. Macerate for 14 days. Agitate daily.

Huitlachoche Tincture

- 32 oz Huitlachoche
- 32 oz Everclear

Combine. Macerate for 24 hours.
Fine strain.

Huitlachoche Vermouth

- 5 parts Boisserre dry vermouth
- 1 part Huitlachoche tincture

Combine all ingredients.

THE LITTLEJOHN COBBLER

Daiquiri Time Out
Recipe: Brad Stringer
2701 Market St
Galveston, TX 77550
(409) 497-2760
dtogalveston.com

I couldn't be happier that Texas has a bar named DTO (Daiquiri Time Out). I also couldn't be happier that it's Brad Stringer at the helm. First at Boheme, then Johnny's Gold Brick in Houston, now he leads Galveston into craft cocktail culture with seasonal menus and a variety of styles for guests to consume. The Littlejohn Cobbler takes its name from Elbridge Gerry Littlejohn (1862–1935), who was one of the great documentarians of South Texas and the author of *Texas History Stories* and *Geography of Texas*. At DTO, the kumquats used in this cocktail typically come from the property where Littlejohn built his home.

Glassware: **Julep Mug**

Garnish: **Mint Sprig, Sliced Strawberry, Sliced Kumquat, Powdered Sugar**

- **1.5 oz Kumquat-Strawberry Syrup**
- **.75 oz PX sherry**
- **.75 oz Oloroso sherry**
- **.75 oz Plantation OFTD rum**
- **.25 oz fresh lime juice**

1. Combine ingredients in a shaker with ice and shake vigorously, then strain over ice in julep mug.

2. Top with crushed ice.

3. Garnish with mint sprig, sliced strawberry, sliced kumquat, and powdered sugar.

Kumquat-Strawberry Cordial

- 1 cup fresh kumquat juice
- 3 cups strawberry syrup
- .75 cup vodka

Cut and macerate strawberries in sugar to make strawberry syrup.

Spiced Coffee Salt

In a small bowl, combine equal parts kosher salt, ground Vietnamese coffee, and dark anchor chili powder and mix well.

SEVENTEEN NORTH

Kâu Ba
2502 Dunlavy St Suite B
Houston, TX 77006
(713) 497-5300
kaubakitchen.com

One of the most interesting cuisines in Texas is Viet-Cajun. It's based on both the heritage of the Vietnamese who settled in Houston and fell in love with Southern-style American food and Kâu Ba is the absolute king when it comes to these flavors. The Seventeen North refers to the 17th parallel, which was the line of demarcation during the Vietnam War, but it also happens to be the latitude of the beloved city of Oaxaca, Mexico. This is veteran barman Chris Morris's riff on a classic margarita.

Glassware: **Nick & Nora**
Garnish: **Dehydrated Lime, Coffee Beans**

- **1.5 oz mezcal**
- **.75 oz fresh lime juice**
- **.5 oz Velvet Falernum**
- **.25 oz Black Sugar simple Syrup (2:1)**
- **2 dashes coffee bitters**

1. Rim the glass with Spiced Coffee Salt.

2. Combine all ingredients in a cocktail shaker with ice, shake vigorously, and roll everything, including the ice, into the glass.

3. Garnish with dehydrated lime and coffee beans.

ALL TAI'D UP

Rye
111 W Virginia St
McKinney, TX 75069
(469) 625-1793
ryemckinney.com

Rye is one of those suburban cocktail joints that is becoming all the rage. With the success in McKinney, they've started expanding, even into the big city. The Dallas location is next door to its sister concept, Apothecary. They are truly some of the most creative and interesting cocktail makers in the state. This Mai Tai (but with bourbon) relies heavily on the house-made Maple Pecan Falernum. It might take awhile to make but it's worth it and you'll be sipping on this bad boy all week.

Glassware: **Collins Glass**
Garnish: **Orange Triangle**

- **1 banana leaf**
- **2 oz bourbon**
- **1 oz Maple Pecan Falernum**
- **.5 oz orange juice**
- **.5 oz fresh lime juice**
- **.5 oz dry curacao**

1. Trim a banana leaf to create a long rectangle and place it in the glass so it is curling upward. Fill the glass with pebble or crushed ice.

2. Combine all ingredients in a cocktail shaker with ice, shake vigorously, and strain into the glass.

3. Garnish with the orange.

Maple-Pecan Falernum

- **4 cups toasted pecan pieces**
- **2 qt water**
- **3 cups white sugar**
- **Zest of 2 oranges**
- **Zest of 4 limes**
- **2 cinnamon sticks, broken**
- **20 whole cloves**
- **20 allspice berries**
- **6 star anise pods**
- **.5 cup chopped ginger (unpeeled)**
- **2 cups demerara sugar, or half white sugar and brown sugar**
- **2 cups maple syrup**
- **2 oz orange juice**
- **2 oz fresh lime juice**
- **1 oz dark overproof rum per 5 oz strained mixture**

1. Place 2 cups each pecan pieces in two 1 qt mason jars, fill with water, and steep until the liquid becomes milky and opaque, similar to almond milk, at least 4 hours and up to 24.

2. Place white sugar in a 1 qt deli container and then, using a microplane, zest the oranges and limes onto the sugar. Using a muddler and barspoon, incorporate the zest into the sugar, creating an oleo sacrum (sugar oil). Let sit as long as the pecan and water mixture.

3. After steeping pecans and letting oleo sacrum marinate, toast the cinnamon sticks, cloves, allspice, and star anise in a 4 qt saucepan over medium-high heat. Then add the pecan mixture, oleo sacrum, and fresh ginger to the saucepan and reduce heat to medium. Bring to a simmer and reduce heat so as not to burn the sugar or boil over. Simmer for 30 to 35 minutes.

4. Strain spices and nuts from the liquid and return it to the saucepan. Over low-medium heat, add orange and lime juices, maple syrup, and maple sugar. Once maple sugar is dissolved, taste and make sure pecan and maple flavors are prominent enough. Allow the mixture to cool and then strain into a large graduated pitcher. Add 1 oz of dark overproof rum for every 5 oz of mixture.

Thyme/Citrus Water:

Boil 2 liters water with 8 ounces thyme, 8 ounces brown sugar, and the zest from 2 limes.

Then strain that and mix with:

- 10 oz fresh orange juice
- 8 oz grapefruit juice
- 12 oz lemon juice
- 16 oz lime juice

CENTRAL STANDARD THYME

Neighborhood Services
Recipe: Ivan J Rimach

5027 W Lovers Lane
Dallas, TX 75209
(214) 350-5027
nhstheoriginal.com

Neighborhood Services is one of the most important institutions in Dallas culinary history. Having multiple locations, one of the biggest influences was the Neighborhood Services Tavern, which was run by famed bartender Jason Kosmas shortly after moving to Dallas. Many a Dallasite has been introduced to cocktails by Jason at Neighborhood Services (including myself), and in a manner similar to the food served, the Neighborhood Service cocktail program has always been about approachability. This cocktail is a simple riff on a pisco sour and is mighty delicious, y'all.

Glassware: **Rocks Glass**
Garnish: **Lemon Wheel, Thyme Sprig**

- **.75 oz lime juice**
- **.5 oz simple syrup**
- **.75 oz Thyme/Citrus Water**
- **2 oz Pisco Cuatro G's Acholado**
- **Ginger beer**

1. Add all ingredients to a rocks glass and stir.

2. Top with ginger beer.

—Caffe Del Fuego—

RFDISTILLERS.COM

Caffe Del Fuego is one of the most pleasant surprises of this journey. This is a coffee lover's dream spirit. It's a five-bean blend of Arabica coffee beans from micro lot farms in Brazil, El Salvador, Mexico, Ethiopia, and Indonesia that contribute to these specialty grade coffees. They work hand-in-hand with the Austin Roasting Company in creating the blend.

The Fuego guys then heat-brew this freshly roasted and ground coffee at a very proper 202 degrees, and then add pure cane dark sugar and Madagasgar bourbon vanilla.

They're the only coffee liquor that uses this method, which is significant because there are 150 flavonoids in heat-brewed coffee and only 25 in cold-brewed coffee. IF you've ever compared cold-brew directly to the same beans heat-brewed, you know what I'm talking about.

Fuego is a delicious, alcoholic, caffeinated coffee... which makes it perfect for day drinking. Frankly, as I write this, I'm enjoying my "Saturday morning coffee" right now, because, 3 oz of Fuego has about 40 mg of caffeine.

Founded in Austin, Texas, in 2013 by cousins Peter and Mark Remington Koelsch and their first spirit was Caffe del Fuego. The name loosely means "coffee of the fire" or "fire coffee" and is an intentional hybrid of Italian and Spanish. Caffe del Fuego is based on a recipe shared by an old Italian gentleman and friend named Vincent who agreed to the use of the recipe with one rule: Don't screw it up.

Peter passed away in May of 2021 and will forever be remembered for his humor and his devilish smile. He was one of the most loyal and entertaining people I met working on this book and I know that I personally miss him terribly. And Vincent… they didn't screw it up.

The South Texan

- 1 oz Caffe del Fuego
- 1 oz quality Anejo
- .25 oz quality orange liqueur
- .125 oz Ancho Reyes
- 2 dashes orange bitters
- 2 dashes chocolate bitters

On the rocks, stirred, and garnished with an orange peel.

BERRY WHITE

Recipe: Devin McCullough, The People's Last Stand

The Berry White is especially tasty if you're looking for a kick of bourbon, but it's still refreshing and not overly boozy.

Glassware: **Red or White Stemless Wine Glass**
Garnish: **Berry Compote, Long Lemon Peel with Bamboo Pick**

- **2 oz bourbon (4 Roses or Old Grand Dad)**
- **.75 oz fresh orange juice**
- **.5 oz fresh lemon juice**
- **.5 oz rich demerara syrup**
- **1 oz Wild Berry Cordial**

1. Combine ingredients in a shaker with ice and shake vigorously.
2. Double strain into wine glass.
3. Top with Berry Compote and garnish with lemon peel.

Wild Berry Cordial

- **2 pints blueberries**
- **1 pint blackberries**
- **1 pint raspberries**
- **1.5 pints brown sugar**
- **8 oz bourbon (4 Roses or Old Grand Dad)**

Cook to a boil or when the berries start to pop.

Chill cordial. Then double strain into a glass bottle.

Berry Compote

Soak wild berries in cognac.

—The People's Last Stand—

5319 E Mockingbird Ln
Dallas, TX 75206
(214) 370-8755
thepeopleslaststand.com

One of the first cocktail-centric programs in Dallas, People's Last Stand is an island of cool in the sea of suburban-esque Mockingbird Station. With alumni like Alex Fletcher (Atwater Alley), Omar Yeefoon (Shoals Sound and Service), Chris Dempsey (D & D Shrubs and Strups), and others, People's Last Stand has played a pivotal role in the ascension of cocktails in Dallas.

PETALS FROM THE PAST

The Hard Shake Bar
211 S Akard St
Dallas, TX 75202
hardshakebar.com

The crown jewel of The Exchange Hall, situated inside the AT&T Discovery District, this is the sister property of Jaxon Beer Garden. The Hard Shake is upscale, elegant, and a fantastic escape while overlooking the entire park. Beverage Director Alex Fletcher and master of curation Adrian Verdin have created intimacy in the midst of a 6.5 acre wonderland in downtown Dallas. Petals from the Past, created by Angela Montesclarlos, is a refreshing yet strong drink that's made for people watching on the balcony.

Glassware: **Double Rocks Glass**
Gsrnish: **Jasmine Flower**

- **1.5 oz La Gritona Reposado**
- **.5 oz Jasmine-Infused Lillet Blanc**
- **.25 oz Honey Syrup**
- **2 dashes orange bitters**
- **1 jasmine flower**

1. Combine all ingredients in a mixing glass, fill three-quarters full with ice, and stir with a barspoon until it begins to condensate on the glass.

2. Strain into a chilled glass, slowly place ice into the drink, and garnish with a jasmine flower.

Jasmine-Infused Lillet Blanc

- **2 cups dried jasmine flowers**
- **1 bottle Lillet Blanc**

1. Combine ingredients in a large mason jar, seal, and let stand at room temperature for 24 hours.

2. After 24 hours, strain into a large pitcher, pressing the jasmine flowers to release all their liquids.

3. Return to mason jar, seal, and keep refrigerated for up to 3 months.

Honey Syrup

- **2 parts favorite local honey**
- **1 part water**

1. Pour honey into a pitcher.

2. Boil water, add to honey, and whisk until combined.

3. Pour syrup into a mason jar, let cool at room temperature, and keep refrigerated for up to 30 days.

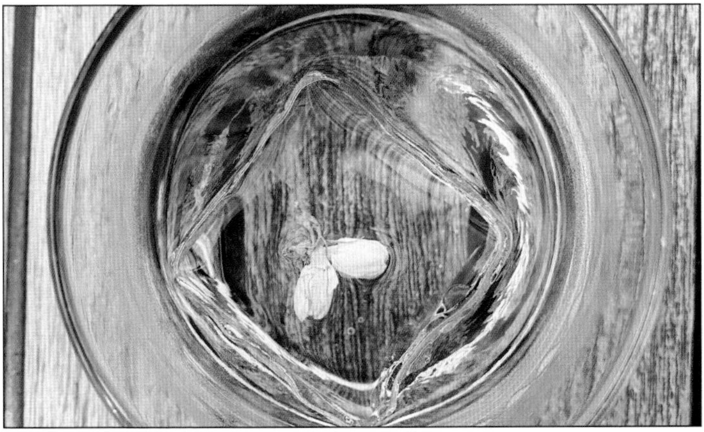

HOUSTON

"HOUSTON'S ONE OF THE MOST DIVERSE URBAN AREAS IN THE ENTIRE COUNTRY, AND MOST PEOPLE HERE ARE REALLY PROUD OF THAT."

—Laura Moser

Everyone who's into cocktails in Texas owes a lot to Bobby Heugel. The story of Anvil Bar & Refuge is well documented. From being the first cocktail bar in Texas to creating the list of 100 cocktails that everyone should try, the evolution of their training program is jokingly referred to as "The University." Anvil is the cornerstone of Texas cocktails. Were people doing it before Anvil? Yep... but that has never been what's most important. It's the structure, the attention to detail, and the fact that it was the spark that started the wildfire that cocktails have become that makes Anvil influential.

Houston has become a destination for some of the best drink makers in the world. The creativity and ingenuity shown in Houston is on par with any scene, anywhere. Houston is one of the top culinary cities in America, and, without a doubt, their cocktail history has played a vital role in its ascent. The fusion of cultures in Houston resonates strongly in the way they go about making drinks. As one of the largest, most diverse cities in America, Houston's cocktail scene is a direct reflection of itself.

While writing this, Hurricane Harvey hit and its impact will be felt from now on. Forever. The estimated cost of the storm is $190 billion. Yes, with a *b*. But we'll recover. Houston will recover. Rockport will recover. Victoria, Port Aransas, Port Arthur, and Conroe will all recover. That's how we're built. Texans are the most resilient people I know. If there's devastation, we bond together. If there's tragedy, we are the support system. If there's anywhere in the world that can take a catastrophic event like Hurricane Harvey and turn it into a rally for a community, it's Texas.

Houston Strong.

—Anuil Bar & Refuge—

1424 WESTHEIMER RD
HOUSTON, TX 77006
(713) 523-1622
ANVILHOUSTON.COM

The quality of bars in the state is directly proportional to the expectation established by our first one, Anvil Bar & Refuge. Anvil has been nominated for or won basically everything from Spirited Awards to local media awards to consistently ranking in World's Best Bars… and throw in being a semifinalist for the James Beard Award for Outstanding Bar Program. This is, without question, the most intense, knowledge-filled training program I've ever seen. Some of those who have made their way through the program literally refer to it as The University. This is grad school, y'all.

PASSING DEADLINE

Recipe: Terry Williams

Anvil Bar & Refuge is dedicated to making the best drinks they can with the highest quality spirits and ingredients they can find. Their dedication to specificity is world-class. This is the best bar in Texas.

Glassware: **Rocks Glass**
Garnish: **Grated Cinnamon, Cinnamon Stick**

- **1.5 oz Old Granddad BIB bourbon**
- **.5 oz Cocchi Torino vermouth**
- **.5 oz Lustau East India sherry**
- **.5 oz Salers Gentiane**
- **1 barspoon turbinado syrup**
- **1 dash Angostura bitters**
- **1 dash Bittermen's mole bitters**

Stir all ingredients and strain over ice. Grate cinnamon on top and garnish with a cinnamon stick.

THE FREEZER MARTINI

Night Shift
3501 Harrisburg Blvd, Ste A
Houston, TX 77003
nightshiftbar.com

Night Shift, a collaboration between award-winning bartenders Justin Ware and Patrick Abalos, is a community-minded bar in Houston's historic East End. The Freezer Martini was inspired by an ongoing discussion among its bartenders about how to go about recreating the best martini they ever had. The answer, as tasted in Josh Bearden's creation, was high-quality gin and vermouth, a series of citrus-forward bitters, and making it really cold—this should be served straight from the freezer, as quickly as possible.

Glassware: **Nick & Nora**
Garnish: **Lemon Twist or Castelvetrano Olive**

- **2.25 oz Tanqueray #10 Gin**
- **.25 oz Hayman's Navy Strength Gin**
- **.50 oz Comoz Blanc Vermouth**
- **2 drops Saline Solution**
- **1 dash Scrappy's Black Lemon Bitters**
- **1 dash Bittercube Trinity Bitters**
- **1.5 oz filtered water**

1. Combine all ingredients in a cocktail shaker with ice, shake vigorously, and strain into a chilled Nick & Nora glass.

2. Garnish with lemon twist or Castelvetrano olive

Saline Solution

- **200 g water**
- **40 g kosher salt**

1. Combine all ingredients in a non-reactive vessel, mix until dissolved, and use as needed.

To really capture the extra-cold emphasis of this drink, make a large batch and place in the freezer for at least six hours; serve it in a chilled glass and garnish the same as if you are pouring a single serving. This batch yields about six drinks.

Liter Batch Recipe:

- **15.75 oz Tanqueray #10 Gin**
- **1.75 oz Hayman's Navy Strength Gin**
- **3.5 oz Comoz Blanc Vermouth**
- **14 drops Saline Solution**
- **7 dashes Scrappy's Black Lemon Bitters**
- **7 dashesBittercube Trinity Bitters**
- **10.5 oz Water**

Combine all ingredients in a glass container with a lid and place in the freezer overnight before serving.

WHITMEYER'S
TEXAS
PEACH
FLAVORED
WHISKEY
Handcrafted in small batches
750 mL
40% Alc./Vol. (80 Proof)

—Whitmeyer's Distilling—

Back in 2003, while stationed in Germany with the US Army, Travis Whitmeyer met a girl whose family had been making alcohol for generations. "When I was stationed in Germany, I started dating one of the local girls there. She invited me over for supper one evening and being a good diplomat, I brought them some Hershey's chocolate and a case of Budweiser. They loved the chocolate and hated the beer," Travis said. They lived on a small Bavarian farm, and turned their surplus produce into various beers, wines, ciders, and schnapps. Travis couldn't get enough of it and decided to study their process.

Once he returned to the US from his tour of duty, Travis started going to the University of Houston. His brother Chris, who was also an Iraq veteran, started attending Lamar University. Travis said, "One of my first business classes, I had to write a business plan, so I wrote one for a distillery. Thirteen years later, here we are." Travis convinced his dad and brother to join him and they wound up raising money from friends and family to start. Whitmeyer's Distilling opened the first legal distillery in Harris County in 2012. Their products are available across the state.

BIRDS & BEES

Miss Carousel
1201 Emanuel St
Houston, TX 77003
(832) 582-7330
agricolehospitality.com/miss-carousel

This cocktail was inspired by the Bees Knees, a cocktail traditionally made with gin, lemon juice, and simple syrup. I wanted something that was bright, floral, and playful. I really love the flavor profile of this cocktail: the bergamot from the Italicus highlights the honey, while the cardamom notes in the Tanqueray and chartreuse create this beautiful symphony of flavors and depth."

- **1.5 oz Tanqueray 10 Gin**
- **.25 oz yellow chartreuse**
- **.25 oz Italicus**
- **.75 oz fresh lemon juice**
- **.25 oz lemon oleo**
- **.25 oz wild honey**
- **.5 oz egg white**

1. Combine all ingredients in a cocktail shaker and dry shake.

2. Add 4 to 7 cubes ice, shake again, and strain into a coupe.

SPIRITS
COMPETITION
2012
DOUBLE
GOLD
FESTLIG
AQUAVIT
KROGSTAD
DISTILLED FROM GRAIN

EARLY START

Better Luck Tomorrow
Recipe: Alex Negranza
544 Yale St
Houston, TX 77007
(713) 802-0845
betterlucktomorrowhou.com

Better Luck Tomorrow is a neighborhood bar with restaurant-quality food from James Beard Award winner Justin Yu. (The party melt is one of the best burger-like sandwiches I've ever had.) Set in The Heights in Houston, Better Luck Tomorrow is a neighborhood bar with incredible food and stellar drinks. This is what the cocktail scene is moving to and it's one of the best things that could happen for the democratization of cocktails. There's been a shift in the restaurant industry away from "a restaurant with great drinks" to "a bar with great food," and BLT is a prime example. There's no 100 list here, even though your bartender will be able to make anything off of it, but there is special attention paid to the affordability and accessibility of the cocktail menu.

Glassware: **Libbey Coupe Glass**
Garnish: **Red Vein Sorrel Leaf**

- **1.5 oz Krogstad aquavit**
- **.5 oz lime juice**
- **.5 oz orgeat syrup**
- **1 egg white**
- **1 french sorrel leaf**

1. Combine ingredients in a shaker with ice and shake vigorously.

2. Fine strain into a coupe glass.

JOHNNY'S BOILER MAKER SHOT

Johnny's Gold Brick
Recipe: Leslie Krockenberger
2518 Yale St
Houston, TX 77008
(713) 864-2424
treadsack.com/johnnys

This recipe may seem a little daunting, but it's one of the most straightforward concepts you'll find in bars. It's a shot and a beer. The beautiful thing about this recipe is that you're making a batched old fashioned, which in and of itself can be fun to play around with. (Try getting one of those tiny barrels and aging it a bit.) Just make sure you double the amount of water, then pour over ice and garnish with orange zest and a cherry. Johnny's Gold Brick, to me, is a quintessential Texas cocktail bar. When you walk in you'll see the doctor who lives around the corner, the mechanic just off work, and everyone in between. And odds are they're both drinking boilermakers… at least for the first round. And you'll have plenty since this recipe is for about 50 ounces.

Glassware: **Shot Glass**
Garnish: **Salt, Sugar, Orange Slice**

- **32 oz Mellow Corn Whiskey (any inexpensive whiskey, the higher the proof the better, 90–100 proof for best results)**
- **10 oz purified water**
- **8 oz orange cherry syrup**
- **1 oz Angostura bitters**

1. Combine all ingredients and mix thoroughly. Bottle in a resealable bottle and refrigerate for up to one month. Serve chilled.

2. Serve in a shot glass rimmed with a combination of salt and sugar in the raw and an orange slice soaked in Angostura bitters.

3. Accompany the shot with a Lone Star beer.

Orange Cherry Syrup

- 8 oz cherry syrup from Luxardo or Armerena Cherries (the syrup is in the jar or can that the cherries themselves come in).
- 1 whole orange (peels only)

Bring cherry syrup and peels to a light simmer, remove from heat immediately, and let cool with the peels in the syrup. If you boil the syrup with the peels it will become bitter.

Strain out the peels and store in an airtight container for up to one month.

— WHAT REALLY HAPPENED —

Recipe: Erik Bogle, Houston Watch Company

A simultaneously playful and reverent tribute to one of Houston's strongest, fiercest, most independent, and successful women. When asked to describe the cocktail, head barman Erik Bogel said "I was inspired by a raw and emotional artistic journey that made intense personal revelations public by way of some of the most bangin' tracks to come out of our fair city. The ingredients represent my interpretation of the story, but like any art, you're free to assign your own meanings."

The drink itself is a bright refreshing palate cleanser. A sunny day sipper that might remind you that a little self-reflection on a hot sunny day in Texas can put you in the mindset to be powerful and achieve greatness.

Glassware: **Collins Glass**
Garnish: **Lemon Peel**

- **.75 oz London dry gin**
- **.75 oz Barrow's Intense Ginger liqueur**
- **.75 oz lemon juice**
- **.25 oz honey syrup**

1. Combine ingredients in a shaker with ice and shake vigorously.

2. Dump container along with shaken (now cracked) ice into a collins glass.

3. Express oils by squeezing, then garnish with lemon peel.

Houston Watch Co.'s honey syrup is made by adding 64% water by weight to standard clover honey.

—Houston Watch Co.—

913 FRANKLIN ST
HOUSTON, TX 77002
(713) 485-0006
HOUSTONWATCHCOMPANY.COM

The Houston Watch Company is located in the Southern Pacific Railroad Building, which was built in 1910. In 1912, Houston jeweler V. A. Corrigan opened his Houston Watch Company in the Franklin Street retail space adjacent to the building's lobby. Today, it's where you can find some of the best drinks in the city in a relaxed atmosphere presented with impeccable service.

—Lei Low—

6412 N MAIN ST
HOUSTON, TX 77009
(713) 380-2968
LEILOWHTX.COM

"You're going to Lei Low?"

"Yeah..."

"Be careful man... You'll love it. It's an incredible time... but we call it getting 'Lei Low'd' around here for a reason."

Lei Low is a neighborhood tiki bar in a strip mall by a tire shop... and once you've been, you may never end your night at a different bar again. Russell loves tiki drinks and honestly, all he wants is for you to love them too. I asked him about the genesis of the Balinese Room #2 and he said "It was named for the Famous Galveston nightclub (and ZZ Top song) the Balinese Room. Growing up in Houston, one spends a lot of time in Galveston. One of Galveston's most famous or even infamous Polynesian Sites was the Balinese Room. It was owned by Bootlegger and Mafia Types and served as a speakeasy, illegal casino, and Supper Club to the rich and famous people in the area."

BALINESE ROOM #2

Why #2? Russell Theode said, "It's #2 because a friend of mine, Alex Gregg of Moving Sidewalk, created another cocktail with the same name, so like in an old cocktail book it's #2."

Glassware: **Absinthe Rinsed Chilled Daiquiri Glass**
Garnish: **Lime Wedge, Star Anise**

- **1 oz Plantation Grande Reserve Barbados 5yr**
- **1 oz Dimmi Apertif**
- **1 oz yellow chartreuse**
- **1 oz fresh lime juice**
- **1 dash Angostura bitters**

1. Combine ingredients in a shaker with ice and shake vigorously.

2. Fine strain into an absinthe rinsed, chilled daiquiri glass.

3. Garnish with lime and star anise.

GARDEN PARTY

Marriott Marquis
Recipe: Nathan Reffell
1777 Walker St
Houston, TX 77010
(713) 654-1777
marriottmarquishouston.com

Nathan Reffell is one of my favorite people on the planet. The vice president of the Houston chapter of the USBG is overseeing the menu at one of the coolest places in the city, especially over the summer. Perched on the sixth-floor of Parkview Terrace, High Dive serves handcrafted cocktails in a resort-like atmosphere. It has killer views with even better drinks. Bonus, this cocktail helped Nate become a finalist in the 2017 Star of the Bar competition.

Glassware: Coupe Glass

- **2 oz Hendrinks**
- **.75 oz aperol**
- **.75 oz lemon juice**
- **.5 oz simple syrup**
- **Muddled red bell pepper**
- **Pinch of black pepper**

1. Combine ingredients in a shaker with ice and shake vigorously.

2. Strain into a coupe glass.

3. Add black pepper and serve.

POISON GIRL OLD FASHIONED

Poison Girl
Recipe: Brian "Hutch" Wayne
1641 Westheimer Rd #B
Houston, TX 77006
(713) 527-9929

According to an incredibly unscientific poll on my Facebook page, one of the largest selections of whiskey in the state of Texas is at Poison Girl in Houston. It's also one of the great American dive bars. You read that correctly, the best whiskey selection is at a total dive. And it's amazing. Poison Girl is "that bar" in Houston. They just hap-pento have copious amounts of whiskey. It's had the "greatest dive bar you've ever been to" vibe since the get-go. It's only been recently that Poison Girl has gotten into cocktails, so while not known for their cocktails per say, the Poison Girl Old Fashioned is a fine version to keep in mind next time you want to make one at home.

Glassware: **Old Fashioned Glass**
Garnish: **Orange Peel**

- **2 oz bourbon (Knob Creek)**
- **4 dashes Agnostura orange bitters**
- **1 dash Fee Bros Black Walnut Bitters**
- **1 dash Angostura bitters**
- **.5 oz simple syrup**

1. Add bourbon, bitters, and simple syrup in a mixing glass with ice and stir.

2. Strain into an old fashioned glass, with one large cube of ice.

3. Garnish with an orange peel.

Rosewater Mix

- 50% red wine/cardamom syrup
- 25% Rose Combier
- 25% orgeat

To make the red wine syrup, mix white sugar and a moderately robust red wine like malbec in equal proportions at room temperature until dissolved, and add cardamom tincture to taste. We do not heat the syrup. The cardamom tincture is just green cardamom infused in vodka for at least three days.

ROSEWATER SOUR

Rosewater
Recipe: Pasha Morshedi
1606 Clear Lake City Blvd
Houston, TX 77062
(832) 224-4182
rosewaterclearlake.com

While working for NASA, Pasha Morshedi spent years collecting and tinkering and finally decided that Clear Lake was ready to enter cocktail culture. Like most of my other favorite bars in Texas, Rosewater is a neighborhood bar. Regulars are learning the differences between styles of vermouth and trying spirits they didn't know existed before Rosewater. That's really, the coolest part of this whole thing. The Rosewater Sour is a quick sipper, so watch yourself. Regarding the recipe, Pasha said, "The Rosewater mix we used to call our secret mix, but we thought that was stupid, so we tell anyone who asks." It's better this way. It's all part of their education.

Glassware: **Coupe Glass**
Garnish: **Rose Tincture**

- **2 oz floral gin (we use Uncle Val's Restorative, but Hendrick's also works)**
- **.75 oz lemon juice**
- **.75 oz Rosewater Mix**
- **Egg white**

1. Build all ingredients and dry shake.

2. Then shake with ice, and strain into a coupe glass.

3. Decorate the foam with a few drops of a red rose tincture.

—A CONVERSATION WITH—
Bobby Heugel

Tell me about Houston. How did Anvil impact the Houston area?

I actually have a specific opinion about that, but I don't know that it's necessarily as cocktail-y as everybody would like. We built Anvil by ourselves, Kevin and I, with some help from Justin Burrow, who quit the job that he had at the time to come help us build the bar. He just showed up one day and he's like, "I quit and I'm here to help." We're like, "Okay, well, we don't really have any way to pay you."

Justin and I actually drove around Houston and bought all the old bottles of Tanqueray Malacca and sold them on eBay. That's how we paid our bills for the last six months of building Anvil.

We really screwed the opening up of Anvil.

We didn't know what we were doing. We didn't think the cocktails were going to be that popular. It was three of us and Kevin and I had worked together at Beaver's but I basically ran the cocktail program and told Kevin what drinks to make. We didn't train anybody, we just figured it out. Then we just got ran over. It was bad. We were trying to learn how to become business owners and doing all this other stuff, we just didn't know what we were doing.

What was going on in the food scene in Houston at the time that you opened?

There were some good independent restaurants, especially around where Anvil was at, which was why we wanted to put it there. There was DeMarco's, which is probably the best Italian restaurant in Houston. Hugo's was down the street, Mark's, which is closed now, was down the street. It fit really well into a nicer evening, but I don't think that the evening was too fancy. It was still Houstonian in nature.

So the neighborhood embodied the vision for the bar.

Montrose really had an independent spirit that fit us well. Poison Girl, which was our favorite bar, was down the street. We used to go there every single day after we finished working on the bar. It just fit and it made a lot of sense.

THE BRAVE

This cocktail, The Brave, first appeared on Anvil's menu. In fact, when I asked everyone (who is friends with me in the bar industry on Facebook) what their idea of a quintessential Texas cocktail would be… I had more than one suggestion of The Brave. Bobby Heugel said, "I think it reflects the drinks and style of service at Anvil. We prefer bold drinks built with rustic spirits, made in traditional ways."

Glassware: **Wine Glass**
Garnish: **Orange Zest**

- **1 oz Del Maguey Chichicapa Mezcal**
- **1 oz Tequila Cabeza**
- **.5 oz Averna Amaro**
- **.25 oz Royal Combier Curacao**
- **3 mists of Angostura bitters**

1. Swirl the mezcal, tequila, amaro, and curaçao in a wine glass without ice.

2. Apply three small, evenly distributed mists of Angostura Bitters to the inside of the wine glass above the cocktail.

3. Flame an orange zest on top.

—The Pastry War—

310 MAIN ST
HOUSTON, TX 77002
(713) 225-3310
THEPASTRYWAR.COM

The Pastry War is Texas' first mezcaleria, serving agave spirits from family-owned distilleries. Named after an 1838 conflict between Mexico and France, The Pastry War celebrates the rich and vibrant drinking culture of Mexico with subtle French details throughout the bar. With owner Bobby Heugel's deep passion for promoting sustainability in agave spirits and his involvement with the Tequila Interchange Project, it's no wonder this selection is the best in the state. As the saying goes, Bobby's forgotten more about mezcal than most bartenders will ever learn.

FAVORITE MARTINI

Tongue-Cut Sparrow
310 Main St
Houston, TX 77002
(713) 321-8242
tonguecutsparrow.com

Tongue-Cut Sparrow is a formal cocktail bar inspired by owner Bobby Heugel's travels throughout Japan and Europe. There are 25 seats. There are no signature cocktails. There are hot towels upon arrival. Tongue-Cut Sparrow is a different universe with elite service and a menu that is only classic cocktails. This is the most precise execution you'll see... There is nothing like this anywhere else in Texas.

Glassware: **Cocktail Glass**
Garnish: **Lemon, Olives**

- **2.25 oz Tanqueray No.10 gin**
- **.75 oz 50:50 blend of Dolin Dry and Noilly Prat Original Dry vermouths**

1. Stir with ice and strain into a cocktail glass.

2. Zest lemon and discard.

3. Garnish with two castelvetrano olives.

—Yellow Rose Distilling—

So the legend goes, in 1836 at the battle of San Jacinto, a woman by the name of Emily West was, shall we say, "occupying" Santa Anna before the Texan army charged the Mexican camp. The surprise attack ensured General Sam Houston's victory and paved the way for the Republic of Texas. She will always be a Texas legend.

Yellow Rose Distillery is in the process of creating their own legacy through whiskey and education. Yellow Rose launched into the Texas market in 2012 as Houston's first legal whiskey distillery. I was excited and a little apprehensive when I went to visit because I had remembered a Yellow Rose Whiskey I had in the past and, unfortunately, I didn't really like it.

They've grown leaps and bounds. This is great stuff, y'all and others agree. They just won best in class at the American Distilling Institute and a Double at the San Francisco Artisan Spirits. There's always been a bit of a controversy with Yellow Rose (utilizing whiskey from outside of the state to include in blends that are marketed by a distiller named Yellow Rose, with Texas all over the bottle… that whole thing) but honestly, since I last had this to now, they've become good whiskey makers. Maybe it's less sourced product or maybe it's just that they're more experienced now, but regardless, Yellow Rose is solid. They are available across the nation.

THIRD COAST MULE

Yellow Rose
Recipe: Houston Farris, Head Distiller/Mixologist
1224 N Post Oak Rd #100
Houston, TX 77055
(281) 886-8757
yellowrosedistilling.com

This simple riff on a Moscow Mule is similar to any Kentucky Mule you'll find, but it's all Texan. It's easy sipping and a great patio drink.

Glassware: **Collins Glass**
Garnish: **Lemon Peel**

- **1.5 oz Yellow Rose blended whiskey**
- **Ginger beer**
- **Coconut water**
- **.75 oz lemon juice**
- **.75 oz simple syrup**

1. Combine ingredients in a shaker with ice and shake vigorously.

2. Strain into a collins glass, filled with ice.

3. Top with equal parts coconut water (no pulp) and Boots (Texas craft soda) Ginger Brew.

4. Garnish with expressed lemon peel.

GREEN CHILI RANCH WATER

Eight Row Flint
1039 Yale St
Houston, TX 77008
(832) 767-4002
agricolehospitality.com/eight-row-flint

When Eight Row Flint opened in 2015, owner, and overall Marfa, Texas, enthusiast, Morgan Weber made sure that the original Ranch Water was on the menu. With the Ranch Water craze, Eight Row decided to dedicate an entire section of its menu to Ranch Waters, like this one devised by Christian Garza. This is a spicy, more earthy version of the original Texas cocktail. This spectacular whiskey bar calls itself a revisionist ice house that celebrates whiskey mash and masa. And the tacos are outstanding.

Glassware: **Pint Glass**
Garnish: **Dehydrated lime**

- **2 oz Senor Mezcal**
- **1 oz clarified lime juice**
- **.25 oz Lime Oleo Saccharum**
- **.25 oz Ancho Chili Reyes**
- **3 dashes serrano tincture**
- **Topo Chico, to top**

1. Combine all ingredients in a pint glass.

2. Fill glass with ice, top with Topo Chico, and garnish with a dehydrated lime.

— WOOSTER'S SOUR —

Recipe: Steven E. Salazar

This is the Wooster's Sour and it's a pretty cool variation on a whiskey sour. So, wait... Why do I often see Angostura or some other bitters on top of cocktails with foam on them? Well, I'm glad you asked! Generally, in this case, the bartender is using the bitters to impact your nose before you even sip the drink at all. The basic idea is that bitters smells better than egg.

Glassware: **Rocks Glass**
Garnish: **Angostura Bitters**

- **1 oz Old Overholt rye whiskey**
- **1 oz freshly squeezed and mesh-strained lemon juice**
- **.75 oz Mathilde Peche cordial**
- **.5 oz Punch alla Fiamma**
- **.5 oz turbinado syrup**
- **1 egg white**

1. Dry shake all ingredients without ice for 10 seconds.

2. Shake with ice for 30 seconds.

3. Fine mesh strain into rocks glass.

4. Top with a dash of Angostura bitters, and use a straw to swirl the ango float into a design.

—Wooster's Garden—

3315 MILAM ST
HOUSTON, TX 77006
(713) 520-0015
WOOSTERSGARDEN.COM

An amazing craft beer selection, paired with an incredibly long menu make for an awesome experience at Wooster's Garden. You can learn a lot about how beverage director Steven Salazar approaches drinks just by perusing the menu. Salazar has an incredible commitment to seasonality that impacts everything in the program.

AUSTIN

★ ★

"TEXAS ISN'T JUST A PLACE ON A MAP...
IT'S AN IDEA IN THE HEARTS OF OUR PEOPLE."

—*George P. Bush*

When Bill Norris took over the beverage program at Fino in 2005, it was the first introduction of classic craft cocktails to their community in a big way. Bill's perspective on cocktails changed dramatically in 2008 when he traveled to New Zealand for the 42 Below Cocktail World Cup. He, along with other industry legends like Charles Joly, Naren Young, and Ben Carlotto, competed in one of the most bizarre and incredible cocktail competitions I've ever heard of, full of different challenges that wound up changing his perspective on how to approach cocktails. Jump back to Austin, and Bill turns Fino into a machine. He's also now internet buddies with Bobby Heugel, and this whole cocktail thing starts feeling like it could blossom in Texas.

David Alan is another one of those Austin OGs who pushed the envelope in every way possible to further the cocktail scene. He has created training programs for everyone from the home bartender to those who have decided to make this their career, and he is also a powerful voice in the media who championed the new direction booze consumption was moving in Austin. His book, *The Tipsy Texan,* was the literary introduction to the Texas cocktail scene. With Bill and David at the helm, the shift in Austin's bar scene towards cocktails was inevitable.

Austin is a relentlessly casual town. More often than not, fanciness is condemned, and this creates a fantastically approachable food and beverage scene. Austin cocktail bars focus on making great tasting, fresh, and approachable drinks for folks in anything from cowboy boots to flip flops. Some very determined people spent a lot of effort to turn Austin into a force on the national cocktail scene.

★ ★

LOVEJOY

There are no cocktails at Nickel City, at least, not by that name. The word has been intentionally left off of all menus and the drinks are all under $10. The Lovejoy is a deliciously balanced blend of Mexican ingredients. For the shrub, follow the simple shrub recipe from D&D Shrubs and Syrups.

Glassware: **Can**
Garnish: **Grapefruit Half Moon**

- **1 oz Altos Tequila**
- **.75 oz El Silencio Mezcal**
- **.75 oz fresh lime juice**
- **.75 oz watermelon prickly pear shrub**
- **6 drops of sea salt water**

1. Combine ingredients in a shaker with ice and shake vigorously.

2. Strain over pebble ice and garnish.

—Nickel City—

1133 E 11TH ST
AUSTIN, TX 78702
NICKELCITYBAR.COM

There are two areas at Nickel City… the main area, and then the pop-up bar in the back. They call it Cash Only, because, well, it is. It's already hosted some of the country's best bartenders, pop-up-style, all for charitable causes. "It's different when you're opening a place where you plan on it being forever," said beverage director, Travis Tober. And Nickel City, while certainly nicer and much more likely to make you a decent Sazerac, elicits the same feelings as Longbranch Inn, which used to be where Nickel City is now, did… and they were opened for almost a century. Regarding the name, Travis said, "It's actually named after a rough neighborhood in Buffalo that was home to a lot of Polish immigrants. Always liked the contrast of the name."

AOSHIMA ISLAND

The Tigress Pub
100 W N Loop Blvd Unit G
Austin, TX 78751
(512) 600-3232
thetigresspub.com

If you want to know where the cool kids in Austin go, check out The Tigress Pub. This neighborhood haunt has remained a little bit of a secret since opening in 2010, despite a loyal clientele. Inspired by owner Pam Pritchard's fondness for the social warmth of English pubs, this female-run cocktail bar is cozy and familial. The down-to-earth team is always concocting creative signature cocktails, and throwing wacky theme parties like 90s Witch Night, Horror con Tiki, or the always popular Romy and Michele themed Galentine's Day. Because of the staff's overall fondness of cats, Pritchard's Aoshima Island is named after a Japanese island known for having more cats than people.

Glassware: **Coupe Glass**
Garnish: **Edible Flower**

- **1 oz light rum**
- **1 oz plum wine**
- **1 oz Fruitlab Ginger Liqueur**
- **½ oz orgeat**
- **½ oz fresh lemon juice**
- **3 dashes Peychaud's Bitters**

1. Combine all of the ingredients in a cocktail shaker with ice, shake vigorously, and strain into a chilled cocktail class.

2. Garnish with an edible flower.

THROWING SHADE

Recipe: Jessica Sanders

This particular drink, Throwing Shade, is a beautiful way to see how Japanese whisky can be accented and not merely overpowered. Owner Jessica Sanders said, "I enjoy drinking Japanese whisky but am also hesitant to use it in cocktails (especially those with citrus) for fear of covering up all the delicate flavors. This sour is spicy and bright and fits in the 'just rich enough without going overboard' family so as to allow the whisky to shine through."

Glassware: **Coupe Glass**

- **1.5 oz Japanese whisky (such as Suntory TOKI)**
- **.75 oz fresh grapefruit juice (Texas ruby red grapefruit is ideal)**
- **.5 oz Zucca Amaro**
- **.5 oz ginger syrup (Austin-based Liber & Co. brand)**
- **1 dash Peychaud's bitters**

1. Combine ingredients in a shaker with ice and shake vigorously.
2. Fine strain into a chilled cocktail coupe.

—drink. well.—

207 E 53RD ST
AUSTIN, TX 78751
(512) 614-6683
DRINKWELLAUSTIN.COM

Jessica Sanders is, unquestionably, the godmother of the Austin cocktail scene, and her program at drink.well. has produced some of Austin's best craft cocktail minds. From drink.well. being named *Food & Wine* magazine's "Top 100 New Bars in America" to Jessica herself landing in the finals of both Speed Rack and the Bacardi Legacy competitions, the reputation is impeccable.

Tito's
Handmade
VODKA
AUSTIN ★ TEXAS

— Tito's —

Tito started it all. He opened the first legal distillery in Texas. He basically worked with the Texas Alcoholic Beverage Commission to craft the laws that would govern future distillers. He, essentially, started the Texas spirits revolution. We owe a lot to Tito.

As Tito likes to say, "everyone thought he was crazy," and that's pretty evident considering that there wasn't even another distiller's permit issued until almost 10 years after Tito. There are currently 108 active distiller licenses in Texas, and 87 of them were issued after Tito had been in business for 15 years. Let that sink in. What was distilling in America before Tito? It was a glimmer.

Tito's is simply Tito's. They have no line extensions. They are not barrel aging anything or secretly working on a gin. They make the vodka that got people to start calling their name in bars across the United States. I've probably consumed more Tito's in New York than I ever have in Texas.

Tito's is simply the success story that all Texas spirits are emulating in some capacity. Tito is the king and for that, craft distillers, specifically in Texas, will always be grateful for the path that he's paved. Guess he wasn't crazy after all.

TITO'S TEXAS TEA

titosvodka.com

One of the drinks that Texans cut their teeth on is certainly the Texas Tea (or whatever you want to call vodka with sweet tea). This tastes like your sophomore year.

Glassware: **Highball Glass**
Garnish: **Mint Sprig**

- **1.5 oz Tito's Handmade Vodka**
- **1.5 oz freshly brewed tea**
- **.75 oz orange curacao liqueur**
- **.75 oz fresh sour mix**
- **Dash of honey**

1. Combine all ingredients in highball glass with ice.

2. Stir well to combine.

3. Garnish and serve.

Tito's
AWARD WINNING
DISTILLED & TIMES
Handmade
VODKA
Crafted in an Old Fashioned Pot Still
by America's Original Microdistillery
AUSTIN ★ TEXAS
Handmade

Texas Grapefruit

If Texas grapefruits are in season, by all means amplify the measure of grapefruit juice in the cocktail.

THE HATCHBACK

Firehouse Lounge
Recipe: Paul Neuenschwander, Asst Manager/ Lead Bartender, Firehouse Lounge, Austin, TX

Craft dive. The idea behind Firehouse Lounge was to create a "craft dive" bar. The building itself was Austin's oldest fire station, built in 1885, and Firehouse Lounge is on the first floor of what is now the Firehouse Hostel. That, in and of itself can come in handy if you happen to go a little too hard. In case you haven't figured it out by now, you're going to find a lot of grapefruit in Texas cocktails. What can I say? We have the best grapefruit on the planet, and frankly, it goes pretty well with agave spirits. Regarding the Hatchback, Firehouse's lead bartender Paul Neuenschwander said, "The drink is definitely reminiscent of a Siesta Cocktail, but appropriately lengthened with our beloved Topo Chico and subtly sweetened for the Texas summer, which is half the year in Austin."

Glassware: **Mason Jar**
Garnish: **Orange Twist**

- **1.5 oz blanco tequila**
- **.75 oz Campari**
- **.5 oz fresh lime juice**
- **.5 oz fresh Texas ruby red grapefruit juice**
- **.5 oz simple syrup**
- **Topo Chico**
- **Orange twist**

1. Shake and strain all ingredients into and ice-filled mason jar.

2. Top with Topo Chico, and add a healthy twist of orange and a straw.

—A CONVERSATION WITH—

Chris Bostick

So, tell me about you man, where are you from?

Born in Corpus Christi, there for six months. All my family grew up, you know, kind of Central Austin. Went to elementary school in Austin. Went to high school in Leander. I was in Austin until '96 when I moved to NYC and I was there until 2001, when I returned to Austin.

Fast forward to 2002 and I started working at Fonda San Miguel. I had worked with Miguel, in New York, and he was back in Austin at that point, so he was like, "yeah, I'll get you the job here." And so, that was a place that I was given this opportunity to take the reins and run the bar program. I had a budget and wrote the cocktail menus and tried to elevate what they were doing.

Then, in the middle of 2007, I moved to LA, kind of chased a gal out there. I worked at the Beverly Hills Hotel doing cocktails at the pool bar, and then also working at 1912, which is like the deluxe hotel lobby bar. But then from there, I severely fractured my collar bone snowboarding in Southern California, and I was out of commission for months, so I started a blog. If I was going to be out of work for six to eight months, I wanted to find a way to stay involved and keep this momentum going.

So what happened?

Well, ultimately I got hired at the Varnish, and that was like everything I had learned up to this point in my career had led me to that moment. That's when I realized very quickly that if I stick with this, it could be the key to opening up my own bar in Austin. And enough, a handful of years down the road, we did it. Half Step was born.

Worth the wait?

Half Step has been the hardest job I've ever done in my life, and continues to be one of the hardest things ever, but the magic happens outside of your comfort zone. So, there's been no denying that Half Step's put me out of my comfort zone on many occasion. That's where you learn.

So, we opened February of 2014.

What was the cocktail scene in Austin like at that point?

It was budding. There certainly wasn't anybody doing our style, you know, there were still a lot of ingredients in cocktails, still a lot of unbridled creativity, which isn't necessarily a bad thing, but I don't think that the hospitality was really dialed in at that point. Half Step was really more vocal about simple, great drinks with amazing service. Simplicity doesn't mean low quality.

What do you mean, specifically?

Simplicity, if anything else, I think is more difficult than ... some people just keep adding on more ingredients until they think it's okay. A little bit of knowledge is dangerous for a young cocktail community. Because all of the sudden, people think that they're experts, and they're armed with this headstrong hubris. We're getting out of that. For a long time, it seemed that Austin was very full of itself, and now we're kind of coming back to Earth and realizing that "hey, good cocktail bars doesn't mean that we have to do everything so complex."

GINGER PALOMA

Half Step
Recipe: Chris Bostick, Owner, Half Step
75 1/2 Rainey St
Austin, TX 78701
(512) 391-1877
halfstepbar.com

When Texas' own Chris Bostick found himself in LA running one of the hottest cocktail bars in the world, The Varnish, he knew it was a stepping stone. (Or a half stepping stone! Get it?) He knew he wanted to come back to Austin and open up his own place, and he knew he had the team to do so. Half Step entered the Rainey Street scene in Austin when it was only speed bars. They saw it as an opportunity to create an unexpected experience for their guest. It's also a bartender factory with some of the best bartenders in Texas coming through the program. This has been ranked among the best bars in the world, and it's incredibly easy to see why.

Glassware: **Collins Glass**
Garnish: **Grapefruit Wedge**

- **2 oz Tequila Ocho**
- **1 fresh ruby red grapefruit**
- **.5 oz fresh lime juice**
- **.25 oz ginger syrup**
- **2.5 oz seltzer water**

1. Shake all ingredients except for the seltzer with 2 tablespoons crushed ice.

2. Pour into a frozen, ice filled collins glass, top with seltzer, and garnish with a grapefruit wedge and a pinch of kosher salt.

— Still Austin —

440 E St Elmo Rd
Austin, TX 78745
(512) 276-2700
stillaustin.com

Still Austin is brand new, but their programs are interesting enough that I wanted to make sure to include them in our list of great Texas spirits. Initially conceived in 2013 by three families, Still is the first whiskey distillery in Austin's city limits since Prohibition. Helmed by head distiller John Schrepel, Still mills, mashes, ferments, distills, barrels, and bottles all of their products in-house. They utilize local grains, limestone-filtered water, and the Texas climate to make their whiskeys.

Still founded a project called the 1919 Heritage Grains project. This is a multi-year effort to reintroduce antique grains that were grown in abundance prior to Prohibition, but have all but disappeared. In 1919, the USDA did its first national grain survey, so we have a very good idea of what wheat was growing in Texas in 1919 and in what quantities. It ends up that most of the wheat growing in Texas back then was soft red winter wheat.

Soft winter wheat also happens to be the right wheat for making whiskey. Lisa Braunberg, one of Still's co-founders, told me, "1919 is of interest to us because the 18th Amendment passed that year, so we like to think of it as the last good year for the American spirits industry. We want to do is go back to 1919 Texas and re-introduce some of the most popular Wheat varieties of the time."

They also offer several unique programs including a DYOB (Distill Your Own Barrel) program, where groups can learn the craft of distilling from beginning to end of the process. Still currently sells new make whiskeys, including New Make (corn, wheat, barley), Mother Pepper Whiskey (Chile Pequin peppers, Smoked Serrano peppers, and aji amarillo peppers), and Daydreamer Whiskey (Valencia Oranges, Tangelo, and Beramont Citrus) that are currently only available at the distillery in Austin, but by the time this book comes out, they'll probably have distribution.

STILL
AUSTIN
WHISKEY CO

CURANDERO

Rosedale Kitchen & Bar
3800 N Lamar Blvd Ste 170
Austin, TX 78756
(512) 729-0052
rosedalekb.com

Rosedale Kitchen and Bar is a neighborhood kitchen with crave-worthy fare. The vibrantly healthy dishes are a mix of American comfort foods and Texas flair, paired with garden-to-glass cocktails, handcrafted sodas, and a wide array of beer and wine from near and far. Lalo Tequila is pretty outstanding and this cocktail created by Aaron Hernandez allows it to take center stage. The Chaveau and Dolin Dry Vermouth bring a nice weight and roundness to the drink. The name of this drink, which translates to "healer," is inspired by the traditional healing uses of aloe and turmeric.

Glassware: **Coupe**
Garnish: **Rose Petal**

- **.75 oz Lalo Tequila**
- **1 oz Chareau Aloe Liqueur**
- **.5 oz Luxardo Maraschino Liqueur**
- **.75 oz fresh lime juice**
- **.25 oz Kaffir Lime Infused Dry Vermouth**
- **drops Turmeric / Sea Salt Solution**

1. Combine all of the ingredients in a cocktail shaker with ice, shake vigorously for 3 to 4 seconds, and strain into a chilled coupe.

2. Garnish with a rose petal, or any available edible flower petal.

Turmeric / Sea Salt Solution

- **10 g turmeric powder**
- **10 g sea salt**
- **40 ml 80-proof vodka**
- **ml filtered water**

1. Combine all of the ingredients in a mason jar and shake vigorously. Allow solution to settle and shake once more.

2. Transfer contents to a dropper dispenser

Kaffir Lime Infused Dry Vermouth

- **750 ml Dolin Dry Vermouth**
- **15 g kaffir lime leaves (roughly chopped)**

1. Combine all of the ingredients in an airtight glass container and let stand at room temperature for 2 days.

2. Strain out leaves and store vermouth in the infusing container.

— Revolution Spirits —

When co-founders Aaron Day and Mark Shilling decided to push forward with an idea hatched six years earlier, they did so because they saw the pending revolution. Coming from a government relations and public policy background, they were just as intrigued with helping build the Texas craft spirits industry as they were with creating spirits. "We got a lot of mentorship with some of the best craft distillers in the nation by swapping our government relations knowledge," said Aaron.

Revolution assembled a team of brewers turned distillers who agreed with their vision for testing the boundaries of spirits production and collaboration. Revolution is a seemingly endless revolving door of experimentation. They make a coffee liqueur with a favorite Austin coffee roaster, Cuvee coffee. They make fruit liqueurs from spent fruit from the famed Jester King Brewery. They offer apple brandy from Argus's hard cider. They swap barrels with brewers, vineyards, whiskey, and mezcal distilleries for their Single Barrel aged gin series.

"Economically, you need to start with an unaged spirit, so we made a gin that we could experiment with that was to be our flagship product," said Aaron. Austin Reserve Gin is a well-balanced gin with botanicals inspired by the terroir of Central Texas. With hints of rosemary, juniper, and lavender, the gin is presented at a 100 proof, which heightens the finish of the remaining ingredients of lemon grass, pink peppercorn, and hand-zested grapefruit.

Their latest release is a fantastic companion to their flagship gin product, as it is the first Texas amaro.

"My great-grandfather ran moonshine as a kid on his bicycle in the hills of Tennessee and I think Mark has a family connection to a rye whiskey that didn't make it past Prohibition," Aaron told me. I'm glad they've "gone legit" and decided to help grow this industry in Texas. Not only are they some of the most creative spirit makers in Texas, but they're on the forefront of legislative changes that will make it easier for all of us to enjoy this burgeoning industry.

TEXAS NEGRONI

Revolution Spirits
12345 Pauls Valley Rd
Austin, TX 78737
(512) 358-1203
revolutionspirits.com

This is as Texas as it gets, y'all. 100% Texas ingredients in this classic Negroni recipe.

Glassware: Rocks Glass
Garnish: Grapefruit

- **2 oz Austin Reserve Gin**
- **1 oz Amico Amaro**
- **1 oz rouge vermouth**
- **Grapefruit peel**

1. Place a large ice cube in a rocks glass.

2. Combine gin, amaro, and vermouth in the glass and stir to combine.

3. Rub the rim of the glass with grapefruit peel garnish.

4. Finish with a small Austin Reserve Gin float.

QUARTZ COMPOSER

Juniper
Recipe: Justin Elliott
2400 E Cesar Chavez St #304
Austin, TX 78702
(512) 220-9421
juniperaustin.com

Located in East Austin, Juniper is a mix of the rich flavors of Texas and culinary traditions of Northern Italy. Since opening in 2015, the neighborhood restaurant has gained attention and support as a rising star in the local community, boasting accolades like "Best New Restaurants" in *Austin Monthly*, and "Top 25 Restaurants," by the *Austin American-Statesmen.* It makes sense as Justin Elliot run programs are known as some of the top cocktail programs in the city. I asked him about the orgin of the name and he told me a story about a Macbook glitching and flashing the words "quartz composer" on the screen. He said, "But one reason I thought it sounded 'right,' is the 'quartz' kind of speaks to the minerality of mezcal, but also the almost shimmery top notes of the anise from both the Sambuca and the Mexican mint garnish."

Glassware: **Old Fashioned Glass**
Garnish: **Mexican Mint Marigold**

- **.75 oz Old Highborn Gin**
- **.75 oz Mezcal Vago**
- **.75 oz canary melon syrup**
- **.25 oz sambuca**
- **.5 oz lime juice**

1. Shake all ingredients and strain into an old fashioned glass over ice.

2. Top with Peychaud's and a Mexican mint marigold.

— Emerald Absinthe —

Texas absinthe is a very real thing. But before we get into that, let's get a few things straight. First, absinthe does not cause hallucinations. You are no more likely to see a giant Pokémon eating your Doritos after drinking absinthe than if you were drinking vodka or tequila. Second, the absinthe in the US is "real" absinthe. The majority of United States brands are made with grand wormwood, and they are usually better than a lot of their European counterparts.

Lastly, absinthe drips are real lighting your absinthe on fire is marketing. This little "tradition" showed up in the 90s (The 1990s, to clarify). Those who resort to this marketing and sensationalism are usually just using vodka with some anise and green food coloring.

Emerald Absinthe is a wine-based spirit steeped with 13 herbs and spices including anise, fennel, and grand wormwood, creating a creamy, lingering finish with notes of licorice and green pepper, and a hint of golden raisins.

After distillation the absinthe then endures a second 10-day maceration of herbs, allowing the liquid to change colors with the natural green color of the chlorophyll. Master Distiller Matt Mancuso developed his blend of select botanicals from traditional, early 19th Century French and Swiss absinthe styles. "It's actually closer to what was made in the 1790s than anything in the past 100 years," said co-founder Jessica Graves.

GREEN GODDESS PUNCH

Emerald Absinthe
Recipe: Jessica Leigh Graves
704 Hwy 71
Bastrop, TX 78602
(512) 766-5090
derelictairship.com

The recipe is for a punch but don't be afraid to just toss Emerald Absinthe in some champagne or prosecco. This punch is light but full of beautiful notes of anise.

Glassware: **Collins Glass**
Garnish: **Mint, Lime, or Cucumber**

- **.5 oz Emerald absinthe**
- **1 oz lime juice**
- **1 oz simple syrup**
- **4 oz Topo Chico**

1. Add absinthe, simple syrup, and lime to a collins glass and stir.

2. Top with Topo Chico.

3. Garnish with mint, lime, or cucumber.

— Genius Gin —

The folks at Genius Gin love gin. They've focused their entire journey around their love of gin... as they say, gin is the only vodka worth drinking. Mike Groener, founder of Genius told me, "Upon researching gin and learning about its fall from fame to the hands of the more neutral alternative, vodka, we quickly realized that not only was gin a large cultural part of history, but it was often misunderstood. A whole world of gins exist; in all flavors and colors."

Genius's Old Highborn Gin, is making quite the impression in Texas. It's a traditional dry spirit with a Texas flair, and, unlike most gins, it's pot distilled to retain deep flavors and oils. It's incredibly fresh with hints of cinnamon, tea, citrus peels, and juniper.

Aaron Kimmel, formely of drink.well., began this cocktail as a play on a classic Corpse Reviver. He also uses Cocchi Americano Rosa, which is slightly more bitter and aromatic than the classic Cocchi. It's almost a light Aperol and is incredibly delicious.

CORPSE IMBIBER

Genius Gin
4202 Santiago St #2
Austin, TX 78745
(512) 710-7907
geniusliquids.com

A classic drink for a classic gin. This is one recipe you should commit to memory and bust out the next time someone tells you they "hate" gin.

Glassware: **Coupe Glass**
Garnish: **Grapefruit Peel**

- **1.5 oz Genius Original**
- **.75 oz Cocchi Americano Rosa**
- **.75 oz fresh grapefruit juice**
- **.25 oz fresh lemon juice**
- **.75 oz Gran Classico**
- **Absinthe spray (Tenneyson preferred)**

1. Pour the gin, cocchi, juices, and Gran Classico into a cocktail shaker with ice and shake.

2. Spray glass with absinthe, or rinse.

3. Strain into a glass.

4. Garnish with grapefruit peel.

Kelsey Caudebec is a former bartender at The Tigress Pub in Austin. She's been a part of the Texas service industry since 2013 and her small collection of poems, *Spirit Forward*, is based on her experiences behind the bar.

Spirit Forward

When I Last Called for the last time
I didn't know it,
Woke up the next day to learn it,
Wish I could take it back.
Sometimes now I unlock the bar
Just to sit inside and feel home again

Good thing is I'm a collector
I dried roses someone brought in
For me in June, I keep faded menus,
Matchbook with a stretching tiger,
Borrowed highball near the sink.
Crinkled note on scrap receipt paper,
Wise thing someone said
While I was making their usual,
It's on its third refrigerator
Its my Friday night hieroglyphs.
Polaroid of me from some slow Sunday,
Easy smile, bar towel in hand,
Dated November 2019.

But let's remember the pulse
Of a barful of hearts.
A relay of "I miss you," a postcard
With familiar handwriting
Eye-level on the walk-in.
A gold plaque on the pine
With a name that shines
Above two date.

The flash and rattle of metal tins,
Tempo of the tavern-keeper
Before icy pour into cold coupes.
Thunder announcing downpour,
Rain curtain from the eaves,
Better get another drink.

I'll give you jeweled liquor from foreign
mountains.
Whatever you want. Cold bottle
From your home state, wine
You might find on your jacket
Tomorrow. A distant clatter,
Low hymn of the ice machine,
Eleven p.m. surge of voices,
The night's elegy for the day
In preparation for tomorrow.
These are vespers.
Drops of whiskey on your lap
And sage and basil on the breeze,
Flare of a match on a midnight patio.

I want to reach over the bar top,
Watch the tide of sunset

Come again across the field
To cover us in rose gold. You,
Stranger and regulars,
The marrow of the bar,
Whose hearts can always stretch
For one more story,
Who see the life behind an ordinary
door,
The promise under the husk
Of a grain of barley.
We live on in postcards on walk-ins,
In stories we tell strangers,
Echoing on tin ceilings.
In hearts of homesick bartenders,
And memoriams on bar tops.
Gleaming gold on loved wood.
Every night the garden lights still click
on at dusk.
I can't wait until I can tell you again
That it's time to leave, I gotta lock up.

I'll see you soon.

TARRAGUEUR

Roosevelt Room
Recipe: Justin Lavenue
307 W 5th St
Austin, TX 78701
(512) 494-4094
therooseveltroomatx.com

Austin's Justin Lavenue is one of the world's best bartenders... Want proof? He won Bombay Sapphire's Most Imaginative Bartender a couple years back. That's reason enough to go to Roosevelt Room. The massive cocktail menu is broken into various eras and the cocktails invented during each. Now, obviously, you could just defer to the Roosevelt Room signature cocktails... I hear there's a pretty decent bartender there. The Tarragueur is a Texas twist on the classic De Rigeuer. That cocktail first appeared in 1927 in *Here's How* by Norman Hume Anthony, otherwise known as Judge Junior.

Glassware: **Nick & Nora**
Garnish: **Tarragon Sprig, Grapefruit Peel**

- **1.5 oz Texas whiskey of your choosing (We like it with Balcones Single Malt and/or Balcones True Blue Cask Strength)**
- **1 oz Texas ruby red grapefruit juice**
- **.5 oz honey syrup (1:1)**
- **1 small (around 1" x 1") grapefruit peel**
- **8–10 Texas tarragon leaves**
- **1 dash saline tincture (1:10)**

1. Shake all ingredients well over one large ice cube.

2. Single-strain into a Nick & Nora glass.

3. Garnish with three sprays of ten-year Islay Scotch, one tarragon sprig, and a grapefruit peel.

EXTREMEGARD

— Fat Ice —

1340 Airport Commerce Dr Suite 200
Austin, TX 78741
(512) 351-6767
fatice.com

Javier Flores is relentless. He knew what his vision was for the company he wanted to start and he didn't give up until he achieved it. He's also one of the most laid back, cool dudes you'll ever meet. Everyone loves Javi. He's the craft ice man.

I know what you're thinking… craft ice? Absolutely. Ice is one of the most important elements of your drink. Unless you're making The Brave, water is in every single cocktail. If I order a Balcones Brimstone and it shows up in a glass, full of sonic ice, looking like a watered down coke… I'm not happy. Neither are you. They need the Ice Man with that Fat Ice. I chatted with Javi about his journey.

What were you doing before you started Fat Ice?

I have been in the service industry for the better part of two decades and I guess you can say I slowly evolved to this. The majority of my time I was behind the bar, but I managed restaurants, waited tables, and was even a DJ for a bit. I worked across the state in all sorts of venues, but my favorite was working in restaurants. They fascinate me and are where I feel I found my focus. Moving to Austin I had three failed attempts at opening a business that had ice involved in some way or another, but never quite got it right. Some people say the third time is the charm, but for me I guess it was the fourth.

I'm assuming you saw an opportunity, but did you have a particular interest in ice before starting your company?

I was an arrogant bartender for a while and always told myself that no one was going to do something better than me. Ice was no exception to that. I traditionally take my drinks neat and drink my sodas and beverages at room temperature when available. So as far as personal consumption, I never really used ice up until recently. When I did first see hand-cut ice was on a R&D trip I took in 2011, and knew immediately that it was something special and really made a difference in drinks and cocktails. I brought it into a restaurant in South Texas that I was running at the time and slowly went from 30 to 40 cocktails in a night to over 250 in a night all served on hand-cut ice.

I loved my hometown, but knew the only way to further my career was to move to a major market and try to stir and shake with the best of them. I moved to Austin and I saw that only one bar had a clinebell machine at the time and that was Weather Up. With many more cocktail bars set to open and none with access to clinebell ice, I saw an opportunity and decided to seize it.

Why is ice important to cocktails?

Ice is important because it really is the foundation to most all modern cocktails. Whether it is used to chill, dilute, or for presentation, ice is involved in the majority of cocktails today. The most common forgotten ingredient in cocktails is water, which is usually incorporated using ice. I like to say that ice is the equivalent to the flame a chef uses to cook; it is the foundation that everything else is built on. I can say without a doubt, cocktails as we know them today would not exist without ice.

What makes Fat Ice special?

This is something that I have to keep asking myself every day and is what pushes me to constantly want to do better and bigger. I feel that over the past year that Fat Ice has been in business it has changed not only the local ice game, but has made an impact nationally as well. High-quality clinebell ice used to be something hard to come by, but thanks to the Fat Ice business model it is more accessible than ever before. Fat Ice currently affects more drinks than any other craft ice or large format ice business in the country. We currently have distribution throughout Texas and have had our ice used at festivals and special events across the country. The pride my staff and I take in the product I feel really shows.

What is your process?

I only cut my ice in a freezer, which sets me apart from most other people. Most people choose to cut ice wet in a tempered environment, but I find this yields inconsistent cubes that vary in size. Fat Ice is cut frozen, packed frozen, and shipped in marine-grade coolers to make sure that the product arrives in pristine condition.

How has the reception been to Fat Ice?

The reception has been better than I could have expected. I knew my friends and colleagues would like it, but I always wondered about the general consumer. I went from being "Javi" to "The Ice Man" in a matter of months. People are excited about the product's accessibility and ease of use, as compared to harvesting and doing the work yourself, which is the other way to get clear ice in your bars. It is really nice to have earned the respect of your peers for something that you have put so much into.

What's the weirdest/coolest ice project you've taken on?

This past year I was asked if I could make a special cut for a certain "Big Game" in Houston, Texas. This is the moment when I knew this product had potential that I had not even imagined yet. Along with being at major sporting events and festivals/concerts, I take a lot of pride in knowing that the best chefs and bartenders from all over the world use my product in their programs. Getting asked by a guy you just saw on *Chef's Table* on Netflix if you could cut specialty ice for his event I would say ranks up there.

—Small— Victory

108 E 7TH ST
AUSTIN, TX 78701
(737) 701-0500
SMALLVICTORY.BAR

Small Victory is weird, y'all. It's in a weird building with a weird door that takes up some weird spiral staircase… but then you open the door. It's shocking how opposite it feels inside. It's cozy and comfortable, cool but not pretentious, fashionable but not obnoxious and that's before you even have a chance to look at the menu. Owner and beverage director Josh Loving has an incredible background including beverage director at Jeffrey's and Josephine House, opening Weather Up, and running Half Step's ice program. And why not? He started at Fino (where the cocktails in Austin began) with Bill Norris.

CAMPARI COLADA

Small Victory feels like a symphony. There are angles and layers that are the work of a perfectionist designing to their exact mies en plas… and it's incredible. This, truly, was one of my favorite cocktails in this book. You've chosen wisely. Make this one.

Glassware: **Tiki Glass**
Garnish: **Orange Slice, Brandied Cherry**

- **3 oz fresh pineapple juice**
- **1 oz coconut cream**
- **1 oz heavy whipping cream**
- **2 oz Campari**

1. Whip-shake without ice and pour over crushed ice in a tall tiki glass that holds 15 ounces or more, and swizzle.

2. Garnish with an orange slice and a brandied cherry.

— SoCo Ginger Beer —

One of the new kids on the block is SoCo Ginger Beer. Beginning in the mid 18th century, traditional ginger beer was alcoholic and made using ginger root, lemons, and sugar to create a light and refreshing beer. SoCo uses those same great ingredients to brew a non-alcoholic version, while keeping true to traditionally strong ginger and citrus flavors. Then they take that and offer a variety of seasonal flavors.

SoCo Ginger Beer is rooted in Austin but also produced in Denton, by brothers David and Benjamin Weaver. Together, they do five farmer's markets as well as wholesaling to local bars and restaurants. David told me, "We were tired of drinking carbonated water pretending to be ginger beer. It took us more than a year, but we've made the real thing from only fresh fruit, fresh vegetables, and organic sugar cane that tastes better than we could have hoped. No chemicals disguised as 'natural flavors'. No preservatives. No high fructose anything. Just clean, crisp beer made with the freshest ingredients we could find."

My toddler highly recommends the Hibiscus version, while I found myself loving the Jalapeno-Lime. That, my friends, is a very easy way to kick your mules up a notch. In fact, here's your recipe to do so.

MEXICAN MULE

SoCo Ginger Beer
4550 Mueller Blvd
Austin, TX 78704
(512) 387-1955
socogingerbeer.com

A simple mule with a bit of a kick. The spice of the ginger beer pairs perfectly with tequila, instead of vodka, in this twist on a Moscow Mule.

Glassware: **Mason Jar**
Garnish: **Grapefruit Slice**

- **4 oz Jalapeño Lime SoCo Ginger Beer**
- **2 oz tequila**
- **2 oz squeezed grapefruit**
- **.5 oz agave syrup**

1. Assemble all ingredients in a mason jar and gently stir.

2. Garnish with a grapefruit slice.

GOMA FASHION

Water Trade
Recipe: Whitney Hazelmyer
1603 South Congress Avenue
Austin, TX 78704
(512) 920-6405

"There has always been a special place in my heart for savory flavors in cocktails as they presented a delicious challenge. Recently, my coworker was experimenting with a toasted sesame tincture, and it made its way into a coconut and rum cocktail of mine, but the texture of the oil needed something more simple to shine through. I decided to fat wash a rye whisky with the toasted sesame oil and throw in a little vanilla, and that was all it needed. I diluted and pre-batched it for consistency, accuracy, and to keep at a frosty temp, because I like my old fashioneds cold. A cook in the Otoko kitchen and I teamed up to make some Angostura candy that you could stir in, but it is best to reserve that for less humid climates."—Whitney Hazelmyer, bartender

Glassware: **Rocks Glass**
Garnish: **Luxurado Cherry**

- **2 oz toasted sesame oil washed rye whisky**
- **.5 oz Giffard Madagascar vanille**
- **.25 oz turbinado simple syrup**
- **3 dashes Angostura and orange bitters**

1. Pour ingredients over ice and stir for 20 seconds.

2. Top with a Luxardo cherry.

— Treaty Oak —

507 BAYLOR ST
AUSTIN, TX 78703
(512) 974-6700
TREATYOAKDISTILLING.COM

When Treaty Oak started, the only spirits being made in Texas were vodkas. "There was some white paper forecasting saying that rum was going to grow rapidly as a category and possibly be the next craze. I don't know if Bacardi paid people to write that, but that obviously didn't happen," laughed Nate Powell, partner at Treaty Oak. Knowing they didn't want to start with vodka and needing something unaged to begin with, they started to make the first Texas rum.

Treaty Oak Platinum Rum was also the first Texas spirit entirely sourced from Texas. They use molasses from the last sugar mill in Texas. "The molasses was actually a byproduct in the process of making sugar and it was an expense. We started buying it and made it a profit center for them, which helped keep them going. It's a really cool story," said Nate. He also told me that he knew of a few other rums that were using the same sugar mill to source their molasses as well.

The first version of the Treaty Oak distillery included a 10 gallon, homemade still, built by Founder Daniel Barnes' father in law, located in a business park in North Austin. They'd take the molasses beer and dump it into the seven-inch opening of the still. Nate told me, "If you can imagine, this wasn't a perfect process. Usually you'd get most of it in there, but towards the end you'd get a little impatient, you'd get some spills going on. Then we were pouring into mason jars... that's how little we got out of it. People want to say small batch or craft and I just don't know if it gets more defined by our process that we went through."

Now, visiting Treaty Oak is one of the coolest experiences you can have in Texas. No, it's not still in a business park. Treaty Oak Ranch is 28 acres and is now one of the anchors on the famous Fitzhugh Road outside of Dripping Springs. Treaty Oak has always been an innovator and they are currently moving into a very experimental version of its former self. From utilizing smoked poblano peppers (infusion is too strong of a word), to a Dripping Spring only botanical gin, to rye versions of all their whiskies, their laboratory series is some of the most innovative distilling happening in Texas.

— HILL COUNTRY HIGHBALL —

The Highball is making a comeback and bartenders are recognizing the skill it takes to serve a great Highball. The Highball first appeared in 1900 in Harry Johnson's *Bartenders Manual.* Highballs have a larger proportion of a non-alcoholic mixer than their base spirit. When made well, they are simple, delicate, and incredibly refreshing.

Glassware: **Highball Glass**
Garnish: **Rosemary Sprig, Grapefruit Zest**

- **2 oz Treaty Oak whiskey**
- **.75 oz rosemary simple syrup**
- **Waterloo Sparkling Water**

1. Stir whiskey and simple syrup in a highball glass with ice.

2. Top with Waterloo Sparkling Water.

3. Garnish with a sprig of rosemary and a grapefruit zest.

Rosemary Simple Syrup

- **1 cup sugar**
- **1 cup water**
- **2–3 sprigs of rosemary**

1. Simmer mixture for 10–15 minutes.

2. Strain and store in the refrigerator.

MAGGIE BAILEY

This cocktail is from Aisling Gammill, who has been at Whisler's for over three years. Maggie Bailey was one of Prohibition's most notorious bootleggers and, in this cocktail, the use of white whiskey (otherwise known as moonshine) is another throwback. If you're looking for a good white whiskey for this, check out Still Austin. Go ahead, make it super local.

Glassware: **Rocks Glass**
Garnish: **Thyme Sprig**

- **2 oz white whiskey**
- **.5 oz Dolin Dry**
- **.75 oz heavy whipping cream**
- **.75 oz roasted corn syrup**

1. Combine ingredients in a shaker with ice and shake vigorously.

2. Pour over ice in a rocks glass, and garnish with thyme sprig.

Roasted Corn Syrup

- **2 cups corn kernels**
- **1 cup fresh thyme**
- **1 tsp salt**
- **1 tsp ground black pepper**
- **1 tsp vegetable oil**
- **1–2 cups sugar**
- **3 cups water**

Preheat oven to 400°F. On a baking sheet toss together corn, oil, salt, and pepper. Spread evenly on sheet and bake for 12–15 minutes, turning a couple of times until the kernels start to turn golden-brown. Remove corn from oven and transfer to a saucepot along with water and thyme. Simmer uncovered for about 15–20 minutes until the corn has released all of its starch and the stock starts to take on a slightly milky appearance. Strain off and reserve the liquid. Measure the amount of stock and add an equal amount of sugar. Stir to dissolve.

—Whisler's—

1816 E 6TH ST
AUSTIN, TX 78702
(512) 480-0781
WHISLERSATX.COM

Whisler's just feels cool, like there are secrets here... or maybe that's just the mezcaleria on the second floor. Mezcalería Tobalá is one of the first bars in Texas to focus on mezcal. Stepping into Tobalá makes you feel like you've been transported to Oaxaca. It's a place for conversation and education through some of the most beautiful spirits in the world.

In a building constructed in 1917, Whisler's was built to bridge the gap between old Austin and new Austin. It is quintessential east Austin... huge patio, live music, food truck in the back slinging killer food... but inside there's a quiet sophistication, and you're just as likely to be introduced to a classic cock- tail you'd never had as grabbing a round of Shiners.

DALLAS/ FORT WORTH

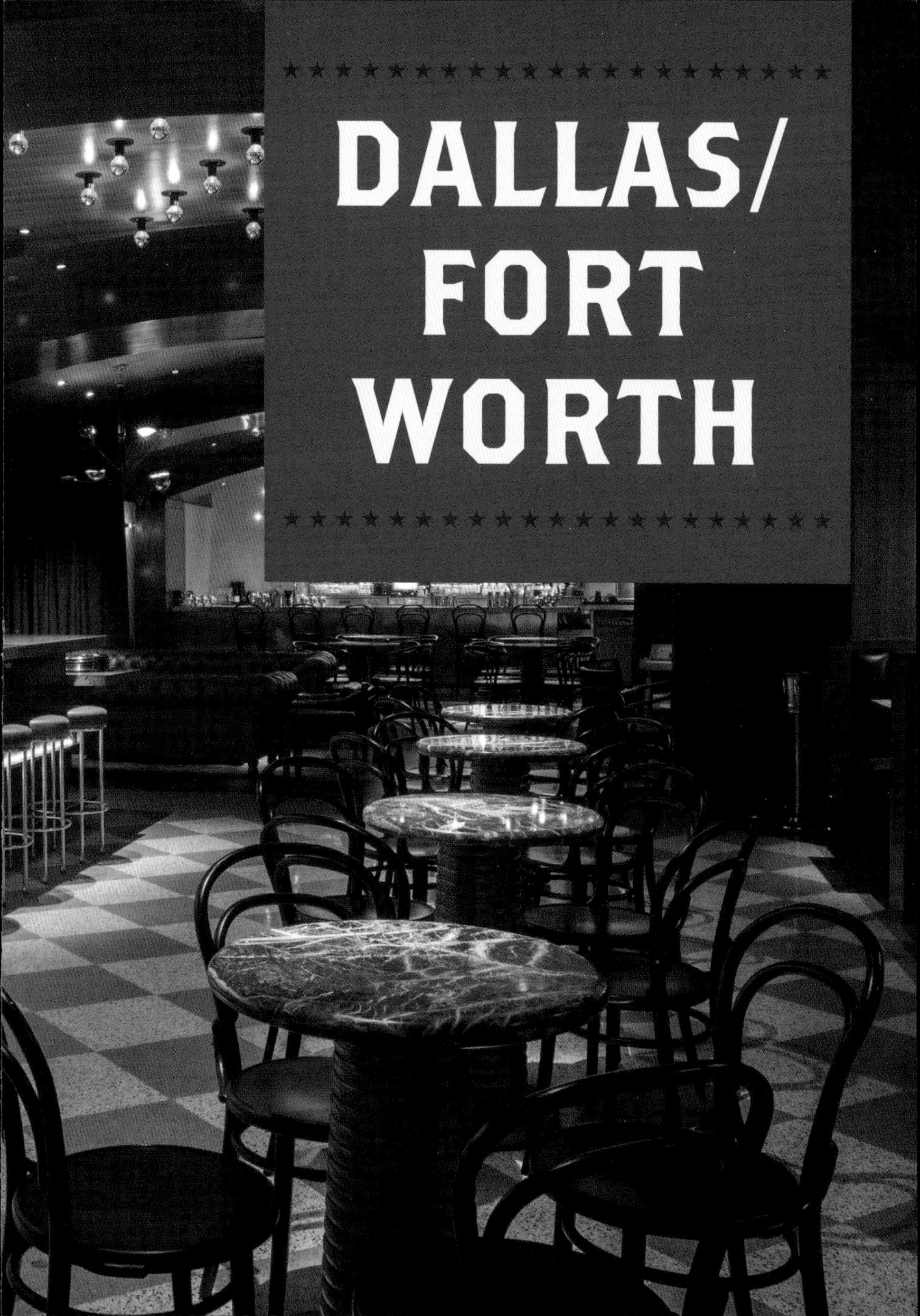

★ ★

"THERE IS NO SUCH THING AS TOO MUCH GOOD WHISKEY."

—*Mark Twain*

Dallas... oh Dallas... I'm from DFW (more specifically the FW part, but I live in Dallas and have for the majority of my adult life) and I can honestly say that it's one of the most fun cocktail scenes in the United States. We have record stores with cocktail bars in them, we have a food truck park that's rocking a Jason Kosmas program, and we have cocktails bars that should be considered among the best in the world. The Dallas/Fort Worth scene is a microcosm of what the Texas cocktail scene represents. It's the epitome of diversity. From the college town of Denton having its own burgeoning scene 45 minutes north of Dallas and Fort Worth, to the great programs in the high-end restaurants of Dallas, to the suburban surge of the craft scene, to Brad Hensarling singlehandedly dragging Fort Worth into the cocktail renaissance... DFW is not only its own thing, but it's also everything.

My favorite aside to the DFW story is the Arcadia Theatre. While Lucky Campbell (the man who would turn Bolsa into a powerhouse, start The Chesterfield with Michael Martensen, and is the current owner of Parliament) was working at The Club in the Centrum building, he was approached about a project to redo the Arcadia Theater. This was 2006 when cocktails were basically only in NYC. As part of the project, the owner of the building flew Lucky to NYC to meet the man he'd be working with on the menu, Dale DeGroff.

The Arcadia burned to the ground on June 21, 2006. Oh, what could have been...

★ ★

THE DAY DRINKER

Blackland Distillery
2616 Weisenberger St
Fort Worth, TX 76107
(682) 268-5333
blacklandfw.com

Blackland Distillery in Fort Worth has, easily, the sexiest, chicest bar I've ever seen in a distillery. It's an amazing place to spend an evening and if you like what you drink, you can walk right out with the ingredients in hand. Megan McClinton's bar program has won Fort Worth's Best Bar. It's not often that a distillery wins such an award. For this, she chose to highlight the twelve botanicals found in Blackland Gin and the shrub itself is a nod to Blackland's owner, Markus Kypreos. The Hatch green chilies add nice heat without being too spicy. If Hatch chilies are not available you can substitute Anaheim peppers in the shrub.

Glassware: **Collins Glass**
Garnish: **Celery Stalk Leaf**

- **1.75 oz Blackland Gin**
- **.25 oz Cocchi Americano**
- **1 barspoon Absinthe**
- **1.5 oz Tomato/Hatch Chili Shrub**
- **1 pinch kosher salt**
- **3 oz Q Tonic Water, to top**

1. Combine all ingredients, except the tonic, in a cocktail shaker with ice, shake vigorosuly, and strain into glass.

2. Top with tonic and garnish with a celery stalk leaf.

Tomato/ Hatch Chili Shrub

- **2 pints organic cherry tomatoes, halved**
- **2 Hatch green chilies, deseeded and chopped**
- **¼ cup white sugar**
- **¼ cup red wine vinegar**
- **¼ cup sherry vinegar**

1. Combine all ingredients in a blender and puree until smooth.

2. Cover and refrigerate overnight.

3. Pour through a chinos and store.

GRAPES OF WRATH

Thompson's Bookstore
900 Houston St
Fort Worth, TX 76102
(817) 882-8003
thompsonsbookstore.com

Thompson's Bookstore in Downtown Fort Worth is quite proud of their history. While the bar opened in 2015, the building was a part of Hell's Half Acre. This was Fort Worth's red light district in the 1800's. In 1910, the building was turned into a pharmacy, then a coffee company, then a pharmacy again until 1973, when it became a bookstore. Today, it's a two story bar, the top being the bookstore and the bottom a speakeasy that feels like a pharmacy. If the blue light is on and you know the password, you're welcome in for a tasty libation. This particular one uses Fort Worth's own TX Whiskey.

Glassware: **Rocks Glass**
Garnish: **Orange Wheel, Cherry**

- **1.75 oz TX Blended Whiskey**
- **.75 oz simple syrup**
- **.75 oz lemon juice**
- **1 oz egg white**
- **.75 oz Chateau Ste. Michelle syrah**

1. Reverse dry shake the first four ingredients and fine strain into a rocks glass.

2. Add ice and float syrah on top.

3. Garnish with an orange half wheel and a cherry.

WHITE ROCK WITCH

Armoury D.E.
2714 Elm St
Dallas, TX 75226
(972) 803-5151
armouryde.com

When they saw an old sign stenciled on the inside brick wall, Armoury D.E. knew they had their name. Since 2015, Armoury has been a vital part of the Dallas scene, and the impact that Chad Yarborough, their original bar manager, has left on Dallas is too large to quantify. Chad created one of the most respected programs in the city and one of the most creative menus you'd see in the state. Chad passed away in 2018 shortly after this book came out. His voice and his spirit still pulses through the streets of Deep Ellum and those of us who got to know him are truly better people for having done so. RIP man... you'll never be forgotten.

Glassware: **Highball Glass**
Garnish: **Orange Zest**

- **1.5 oz Devils River whiskey**
- **.75 oz Amico amaro**
- **.75 oz lemon**
- **.75 oz cappilaire syrup**

1. Combine ingredients in a shaker with ice and shake vigorously.

2. Strain into a highball glass.

3. Garnish with orange zest.

—Western Son Distillery—

If you're a small Texas town, like Pilot Point (50 miles north of Dallas,) when a distillery opens in your town, it's a pretty big deal. Western Son started in an industrial area outside of Dallas, but they grew so quickly that they had to uproot the entire operation and they landed in Pilot Point.

They secured a 30,000 sq. ft. building just 300 yards from the downtown square and five minutes from Lake Ray Roberts. The new location has a live music stage, massive front patio, beautiful tasting room, and lounge. They also upgraded their distilling equipment, including the addition of an Artisan Still Designed 650 gallon pot still.

Western Son has also started brewing beer, under the name Whistle Post Brewing Company. The idea was to create an experience that anyone could enjoy. With rotating BBQ trailers and food trucks, Saturdays at Western Son have become an event. Ta dah! Vodka/Whiskey Tourism!

Funny note… the nickname of the building is "The Old Panty Factory." Built in the 1960s, during the 70s and 80s the Russell-Newman Clothing Company and their primary products were bikini bottoms, briefs, and lingerie. Instead of getting their panties in a wad, Western Son embraced this history and made one of the bathrooms a shrine to commemorate the building's historic past. On one wall reads a quote from a local resident, "My mother-in-law worked here and my father-in-law worked at the GM seat upholstery factory. He used to say they were both in the seat covering business."

Western Son Distillery manufactures Western Vodka, Western Son Gin, and Red River Whiskey, including Red River Bourbon and is distributed in over 20 states across the United States.

BERRIES FROM THE WEST

Western Son
217 W Division St
Pilot Point, TX 76258
(940) 324-0008
westernsondistillery.com

This is one of the house cocktails you can try when you head to Pilot Point to visit the distillery. It's a pretty awesome time.

Glassware: Rocks Glass

- **2 oz Western Son blueberry vodka**
- **1 oz simple syrup**
- **1 oz fresh lemon juice**

1. Combine ingredients in a shaker with ice and shake vigorously.

2. Strain into a rocks glass.

3. Float pinot noir on top.

Pisco, in case you aren't familiar, is a brandy distilled from grape-like cognac. However, to be called pisco, the spirit must be made from grapes grown in specific areas of Peru and Chile and distilled to proof. It works as a great gin substitution in negronis and gimlets. My favorite available in the United States is Campo de Encanto's Grand and Noble Pisco, but if it's not available, Pisco Porton should be and it's fabulous.

OLGA BREESKIN

Bottled in Bond
Recipe: Hector Zavala
5285 Dallas Pkwy Ste. 420
Frisco, TX 75034
(469) 731-5410

bottledinbondparlour.com

Named after the Bottled in Bond Act of 1897, Bottled in Bond is a great example of how cocktail culture is moving into the suburbs. Suburban areas like Frisco near Dallas, or Clear Lake near Houston, typically have plenty of farm-to-table restaurants, but cocktail-driven beverage programs are fairly new. They are the future, my friends. After training in the city centers, the suburban cocktails are the next big trend in Texas.

Glassware: **Coupe Glass**
Garnish: **Chile Pepper**

- **2 oz pisco**
- **.75 oz lemon**
- **.75 oz ancho chile demerara**
- **.5 oz egg white**

1. Combine all ingredients and dry shake without ice for 10 seconds.

2. Shake with ice for 30 seconds.

3. Fine mesh strain into a coupe glass.

4. Garnish with a dried chile pepper.

EVERYBODY'S GIRL

Lounge Here
Recipe: Brad Bowden
9028 Garland Rd
Dallas, TX 75218
(214) 238-3374
theloungehere.com

This drink is as easy drinking and as laid back as the neighborhood that surrounds this cocktail haven. This is one of the most endearing neighborhood bars in the state and their cocktail program is thriving. This drink, featuring Austin's own Highborn Dry Gin, was put on the original menu by Brad Bowden.

Glassware: **Collins Glass**
Garnish: **Grapefruit Peel**

- **.75 oz Highborn Texas Dry Gin**
- **.75 oz St Germaine**
- **.75 oz Lustau Fino Sherry**
- **.75 oz grapefruit**
- **.25 oz lemon juice**
- **Top with prosecco**

1. Combine ingredients in a shaker with ice and shake vigorously.
2. Strain into a collins glass.
3. Top with prosecco and garnish with a grapefruit peel.

Lounge Here

Let's continue the neighborhood trend, shall we? Lounge Here is one of the coolest-looking bars you'll ever encounter. It's kind of a cross between West Texas and Palm Springs, with obvious nods to both vast deserts and 70s airport lounges… in a great way. It's becoming an East Dallas staple, which thrills me since I live here and we were in need of some killer libations in this part of town.

Kevin Gray: Cocktail Enthusiast

Kevin Gray is a native Texan who fell in love with cocktails during a three-year stay on the east coast. In 2009, he founded the drinks website, Cocktail Enthusiast, which became one of the most influential cocktail-based media outlets in the United States. We're glad that he calls Texas home. I had a chance to chat with him about his entry into this whole cocktail thing...

Why Cocktail Enthusiast?

When I started the site, I had just recently discovered good drinks. Cocktail Enthusiast was my creative, and healthier, outlet for exploring that newfound interest. As the name implied, I was an enthusiast—not an expert. Since then I've spent countless hours learning about drinks, their history, and the people and places that make them. And Cocktail Enthusiast is now Bevvy—the San Francisco-based site acquired CE in 2017. We're still focused exclusively on good drinking.

Where did the interest in cocktails come from?

I've always loved to eat. Not just for sustenance, but for sport. Give me the best, weirdest, most unique thing you've got, and I want to eat it. So, it was pretty easy to apply that same attitude toward drinks, especially as bars began to approach cocktails with more of a culinary- and craft-based mindset.

How is the cocktail landscape different on the coasts than it is in Texas?

The craft cocktail movement in the U.S. really began on the coasts, New York and San Francisco in particular. As it trickled its way into Texas, the community here embraced better drinks. First, we emulated what we saw elsewhere, but soon Texas bartenders blazed a trail of their own. Over the past decade, the number of bars in Texas serving craft cocktails has expanded dramatically. Before, you knew of one or two bars in each major city, and you'd have to ask for a particular bartender you could trust. Now, good drinking has been normalized, and not just at the fancy cocktail-centric bars. These days, you've got a good chance of finding a well-made Negroni on the menu of a downtown bistro, and a perfectly stirred Sazerac at a suburban steakhouse. Hell, even a lot of sports bars can make you a decent Old Fashioned these days.

What are your current projects?

I'm currently leading the editorial charge at Bevvy, and I write about drinks, food, and travel for a variety of other websites and magazines. I try to visit as many distilleries and bars as I can. It's a fun job. And while the well-stocked liquor cabinet is a nice perk, the best part about covering this industry is meeting all the hardworking people behind these products and places.

Okay, last one: what immediately comes to mind when I say the phrase "Texas cocktails"?

Texas cocktails can be as diverse as the state itself. We're largely influenced by our neighbors to the south, but Texas draws residents from all over the country and the world, and our cocktail scene reflects that fact. That said, a true "Texas cocktail" might include ingredients indigenous to the region—there's nothing better than a perfectly ripe Texas-grown grapefruit or peach—and one of our many and constantly increasing local spirits, from bourbon and single malt whiskey to sotol.

SUMMER ON THE RIVIERA

Proper
Recipe: Lisa Little-Adams, Proper 2014
409 W Magnolia Ave
Fort Worth, TX 76104
(817) 984-1133

Proper is on one of the most happening streets in Fort Worth, Magnolia. They are a contemporary cocktail bar with a comfortable atmosphere inside and a quaint patio for relaxing under the stars with your pups and your pals. They're another example of great cocktails in Fort Worth. Fort Worth, in my opinion, is the most underrated cocktail scene in Texas. Not nearly enough attention is paid to my home town, and I promise you that the drinks in Cowtown rival any in the state. This summery drink is a riff on a gin sour and is as crowd pleasing as a good honky-tonk band at Billy Bob's on a Friday night.

Glassware: **Coupe Glass**
Garnish: **Lemon Twist**

- **2 oz Citadell gin**
- **.5 oz Bitter Truth elderflower liquor**
- **.5 oz lemon juice**
- **.5 oz Ferrand dry curacao**
- **.25 oz simple syrup**

1. Combine ingredients in a shaker with ice and shake vigorously.

2. Strain into a coupe glass.

3. Garnish with a lemon twist.

ORANGE JULIUS CAESAR

Apothecary
1922 Greenville Ave
Dallas, TX 75206
(972) 850-9192
apothecary.bar

What I love the most about Apothecary is that when they tell you a drink tastes like something, you really need to believe them. Taking over the former Wah Wah Room space in the former Billiard Bar space, this small, swanky cocktail lounge is at the top of the game in Dallas. Blue cheese washed mezcal that comes with a white chocolate cricket? Got it. Hollandaise washed bread crumb vodka in the Oyster Rockefeller shot? Yep. And this beauty that's somehow a flavor combination of an Orange Julius, (yes, the one from the mall), a Caesar salad, a clam Bloody Mary? Believe them.

This recipe has been adapted under the assumption that you don't own a centrifuge, but if you have your own cocktail or science lab, please, by all means, do it the right way. Using a centrifuge allows you to separate flavors from textures and makes this cocktail possible. If you're making it at home without clarifying, keep in mind the texture is not exactly going to be the same.

Glassware: **Coupe Glass**
Garnish: **pickled onion and cherry tomato**

- 2 oz Clarified Orange Juice
- 1 oz Clarified Clamato
- .5 oz simple syrup
- .25 oz fresh lemon juice
- 1.5oz Mizu Barley Sochu
- 1 barspoon Greek yogurt

1. Combine all ingredients in cocktail shaker with ice, shake vigorously, and strain into glass.

2. Garnish with pickled onion and cherry tomato.

Clarified Orange Juice

Squeeze orange juice and then pour juice into a fine-mesh strainer lined with 2 coffee filters.

Clarified Clamato

Freeze the Clamato and then defrost through a fine-mesh strainer lined with a coffee filter.

— THE NOMAD —

Atlas
408 N Bishop Ave #101
Dallas, TX 75208
(214) 983-8510
atlasbishoparts.com

The team behind Atlas is truly a Who's Who of Dallas bartenders. The menu takes guests on a tour of world flavors, artfully curated to allow you to meander. Despite the world travel concept, Atlas is a neighborhood joint that welcomes one and all. Jesse Powell's aptly named Nomad is light, refreshing, and floral and embodies everything to beat the Texas heat.

Glassware: **Collins Glass**
Garnish: **Makrut leaf**

- **2 oz Makrut-Infused Townes Vodka**
- **.5 oz simple syrup**
- **.5 oz fresh lime juice**
- **1.5 oz unsweetened coconut milk**
- **2 dashes Scrappy's Lavender Bitters**
- **1.5 oz JP Chenet Brut Sparkling Wine**

1. Combine all ingredients, except the sparkling wine, in a cocktails shaker with ice, shake vigorously, and strain into the glass.

2. Add ice to the cocktail, top with sparkling wine, and garnish with makrut leaf.

Makrut Infused Townes Vodka

1. In a container with a lid, combine 10 g Makrut lime leaves with 1 liter Townes Vodka.

2. Let sit at room temperature for 24 hours.

3. Strain and store.

–D&D Shrubs– and Syrups

DDSHRUBSNSYRUPS.COM

Chris Dempsey's desire to make the best shrubs in Texas started when he was working in the beverage program at the Four Seasons in Las Colinas, just outside of Dallas. There he met his business partner, Chef Brandon Drew, who started using his shrubs in his cooking and told Chris that he should sell them. After a few of his regulars said the same thing, he started thinking about the lack of quality mixers on the market made with fresh ingredients.

In December of 2015, Brandon and Chris started D&D Shrubs and Syrups and now make 16 core flavors. The Blackberry Shrub, was an essential element in the cocktail that propelled Chris to the National Finals of the Copper & Kings Mixt&pe Cocktail Competition.

If you are in Dallas, you can find D&D at various events, including every weekend at the Dallas Farmers Market,and also purchase products on their website. Chris was cool enough to provide us with two shrub recipes... the right one and the fast one.

How to make Blackberry Beet Shrub (the right one)

Cold press 1 lb blackberries

Cold press 1 lb beets. These should give you between 28-34oz juice each.

Add 30 oz organic Apple Cider Vinegar.

You should have a total of 64 oz liquid. To this add 25 oz honey to sweeten. For longer shelf life, add 2 tbsp citric acid. Strain and bottle. Store in cool, dark place or refrigerate up to one year. Flavors will mellow over time, so the sooner you use it the better it is.

How to make a shrub quickly (the fast one)

1 lb fruit

1 cup sugar or honey

1 cup organic apple cider vinegar

Put all into a pot and bring to a light boil; simmer until berries burst. Turn off heat and let sit for 15 minutes. Fine strain and bottle.

CLEAN-CUT-KID

Hide
Recipe: Scott Jenkins, John Ruiz, Trey Buquoi
2816 Elm St
Dallas, TX 75226
(214) 396-8050
hide.bar

When Hide in Dallas opened, it immediately rivaled every other cocktail bar in the area. Their use of technology and gastronomy allows a different level of creativity than most other bars in Texas. Head Barman Scott Jenkins is a self-taught cocktail nerd who took a specific liking to Dave Arnold's (Liquid Intelligence) style and decided to base his program on molecular mixology. Innovative, yet approachable, Hide is an experience that feels like it could live in any city in the world. The Clean-Cut-Kid is one of their simple cocktails... namely because I didn't feel like writing "now go buy a centrifuge" in any of the recipe directions.

Glassware: **Cocktail Glass**
Garnish: **Lemon Peel**

- **2.5 oz rye whiskey (90% or above rye mash)**
- **.375 oz Suze**
- **2 dashes black walnut bitters**
- **.25 oz Solera-aged Coconut-White balsamic vinegar**
- **3 dashes lemon-coriander tincture**

1. Stir all ingredients.

2. Strain into a chilled cocktail glass.

3. Express a lemon peel over the top and serve.

—Herman Marshall—

Fifteen years ago at a neighborhood coffee shop, a small group of friends would gather on weekends for coffee. Nobody really remembers when whiskey became the subject of debate, but once it did nothing else was discussed with the same intensity. Over the next four years all the ideas and plans for a Texas distillery were put to paper.

When a tightknit group of friends with mutual interests come together to start a project, every now and then, you have a perfect storm of overlapping talents and resources that meld into something truly special. Or the other ten dudes bail. That's when Herman Beckley and Marshall Louis's partnership solidified. They had the plans, but now, they needed to start making whiskey.

Marshall hails from a winemaking family from Cape Town, South Africa, and Herman, from the corn belt of Indiana. With their powers combined, they created a line of whiskeys that rival anything in the state. Even so, the whiskeys were under the Texas radar until their bourbon took a silver medal at the 2013 American Distilling Institute's Spirit Competition. "That's when the distributors started paying attention and wanted to sign us up," said Russel Louis, Herman Marshall's VP.

From the beginning, Herman and Marshall have been set on adhering to the historical methods of production. "We make very simple uncomplicated recipes, with very simple, uncomplicated technique, which is how whiskeys was made in the late 1700s and early 1800s," said Herman. Most of the corn for their bourbon and single-malt whiskies is grown in the McKinney area, with supplemental harvests coming from the Texas Panhandle. And their rye and barley comes from North Dakota. Herman Marshall is available statewide.

PINK CAMPARI

Herman Marshall
803 Shepherd Dr
Garland, TX 75042
(469) 298-3903
dallasdistilleries.com

This is a great balance of bitter and sweet. The Campari pairs beautifully with the spiciness of the Herman Marshall rye.

Glassware: **Martini Glass**
Garnish: **Raspberries, Lime Twist**

- **1 oz Campari**
- **1 oz HM rye whiskey**
- **4-5 fresh raspberries**
- **Splash of pear and cranberry juices**
- **Splash of sweet and sour mix**

1. Combine ingredients in a shaker with ice and shake vigorously.
2. Strain into a chilled martini glass.
3. Garnish with skewered raspberries and lime twist.

THE WOODWARD

Jaxon Texas Kitchen and Beer Garden
311 S Akard St
Dallas, TX 75202
(214) 838-1422
jaxonbeergarden.com

Jaxon Beer Garden is truly an oasis in the midst of the chaos of the fifth largest city in the United States. This cocktail by Aaron Surma features Grayson, the greatest whiskey on the planet. Full disclosure, it's my whiskey.

Glassware: **Coupe Glass**
Garnish: **Dehydrated Citrus**

- **2 oz Grayson Blended Texas Bourbon**
- **¾ oz Combier Apricot Liqueur**
- **¼ oz Fernet Branca**
- **1 barspoon Luxardo cherry**
- **3 Dashes Bittemans' Xocolatl Mole Bitters**
- **1 orange peel**

1. Fill the glass with ice and set aside.

2. Combine all ingredients, except the orange peel, in a mixing glass, fill three-quarters full with ice, and use a barspoon to stir cocktail until it begins to condensate on the glass.

3. Empty ice from the chilled glass and then strain cocktail into chilled glass.

4. Express orange peel over the cocktail and then discard the peel. Garnish with dehydrated citrus.

ONE OF THESE NIGHTS

Jettison
Recipe: George Kaiho
1878 Sylvan Avenue
Dallas, TX 75208
(214) 238-2643

Jettison is a project brought forth by the good people at Houndstooth Coffee. When Jettison was opening, part of the concept of the bar was to do a coffee-influenced cocktail, using coffee as a part of the cocktail but not as the dominant ingredient. According to bar manager George Kaiho, "This cocktail started from a concept of cognac as a base with coffee, amaro, and orgeat involved. As I tried the combination, I liked it more with Amaro, Lucano and less cognac, and eventually the ratio flipped, being Lucano as a base and cognac to support the alcohol." George also won an Amaro Lucano cocktail competition with this recipe. Try this and you'll understand why.

Glassware: **Coupe Glass**
Garnish: **Star Anise**

- **1.25 oz Amaro Lucano**
- **.75 oz Hennessy VS cognac**
- **.25 oz Pierre Ferrand dry curacao**
- **.25 oz lemon juice**
- **.5 oz house orgeat (from real almonds)**
- **.75 oz uncut cold brew coffee from Houndstooth Coffee**
- **Dash Paychaud's bitters**

1. Combine ingredients in a shaker with ice and shake vigorously.

2. Fine strain into a coupe glass and garnish with torched star anise.

FREDO IN CUBA

Midnight Rambler
1530 Main St, Dallas, TX 75201
(214) 261-4601
midnightramblerbar.com

Gabe Sanchez, formerly from Black Swan Saloon, has a customer-first style that has only improved this underground cocktail lair, thanks in great part to lead bartender Haley Merritt. Fredo in Cuba is a classic daiquiri riff, combining funky and tropical flavors of Agricole rhum and banana liqueurs: the Giffard banana adds a rich caramelized flavor, while the 99 Bananas ups the boozy-ness and brings a touch of 90s nostalgia.

Glassware: **Coupe Glass**
Garnish: **Tiny Sandwich Bag Filled with Banana Candy**

- **1.25 oz Clement Canne Bleue Agricole Rhum (50%)**
- **.5 oz Giffard Banane Liqueur**
- **.5 oz 99 Bananas Liqueur**
- **.5 oz demerara syrup**
- **.75 oz fresh lime juice**

1. Combine all ingredients in a cocktail shaker with ice, shake vigorously, and strain into the glass.

2. Garnish with the candy-filled bag.

BURNT SAGE SOUR

Standard Pour
2900 McKinney Ave
Dallas, TX 75204
(214) 935-1370
tspdallas.com

The Standard Pour is the bar that you go to in Dallas to find out which bars you need to go to in Dallas. The bartenders that have come through their program are some of the best in the state. Co-founder Brian McCullough is one of the most influential bartenders in Dallas, and his consulting and event work, is one of the reasons that the cocktail scene in North Texas has blossomed. When you look at the Burnt Sage Sour, the first thing you notice a pretty large amount of Ancho Reyes. This is a wonderful spirit made from Ancho chiles. Brian said, "It has a vast array of cocktail applications aside from just being delicious by itself. So it is a natural evolution for this to be a Texas favorite amongst us cocktail folks." Toss in some overproof rum and you have yourself a splendid sour. This also works well with agave spirits.

Glassware: **Nick & Nora**
Garnish: **Sage Leaf**

- **1 oz Ancho Reyes**
- **1 oz Plantation O.F.T.D. rum**
- **1 oz pineapple juice**
- **.5 oz lime juice**
- **1 oz burnt sugar syrup**
- **3 sage leaves**

1. Shake all ingredients, saving one sage leaf for garnish, and double strain into Nick and Nora glass.

2. Place sage on top and simply brulee the sage leaf on top of cocktail (flame the sage leaves briefly with butane torch—be careful!).

OAXAC THE LINE

Las Almas Rotas
3615 Parry Ave
Dallas, TX 75226
(972) 685-5666
lasalmasrotas.com

Las Almas Rotas is the best mezcaleria in Texas. That means, it might just be the best mezcaleria outside of Mexico. This is one of the best bars you'll ever visit and an experience that truly cannot be matched. Their cocktails are incredible, but their mezcal selection and their authentic food make this a must vist. The coolest ingredient in Jillian Whitlow's Oaxac the Line is the Damiana, which is a Mexican herbal liqueur, known for its aphrodisiacal properties, which means this is the perfect after dinner drink, if you know what I mean.

Glassware: **Coupe Glass**
Garnish: **Expressed Orange Peel**

- **2oz Rey Campero Espadin**
- **1oz Damiana Liqueur**
- **¾oz Cocchi Torino**
- **2 dashes orange blossom water**
- **2-3 drops saline solution (320 g sea salt: 3 L warm water)**

1. Combine all ingredients in a cocktail shaker with ice, shake vigorously, and strain into glass.

2. Garnish with an expressed orange peel.

—Parliament—

2418 ALLEN ST
DALLAS, TX 75204
(469) 804-4321
PARLIAMENTDALLAS.COM

Eddie "Lucky" Campbell is one of the pillars of the Dallas cocktail community. Lucky is one of the first people in Dallas to help spark the city's path towards the cocktail Renaissance. After starting things at Bolsa, Lucky moved into a partnership with Micheal Martensen and created The Chesterfield. Over a hundred drinks on the menu, very focused on craft, and one of the first times Dallas had a bar open specifically to serve craft cocktails. It's since gone, but his new project, Parliament, has the same progressive spirit. Lucky's eye for innovation lives here and it's one of the best in town.

THE SMOKING GUN

Parliament is an uptown Dallas neighborhood cocktail bar that doubles as an industry haunt. It churns out talented bartender after talented bartender and will be important to this city for years to come. This is an impressive cocktail to serve, and once you start smoking cocktails, be careful, because it's awfully addicting. This is a Lucky Campbell original and it's fabulous.

Glassware: **Old Fashioned Glass**
Garnish: **Luxardo Cherries**

- **.5 oz orgeat syrup**
- **3 dashes Angostura bitters**
- **1 orange peel squeezed to release the oils into the mix**
- **.5 oz water**
- **2 oz vanilla infused bourbon**
- **.5 oz Averna Amaro**

1. Stir all ingredients and pour into a decanter. Smoke with cherry wood. Swirl to infuse smoke into cocktail.

2. Slowly pour over a large piece of ice in an old fashioned glass.

3. Garnish with Luxardo cherries.

TX

– Firestone and Robertson –

Founded in 2010 by Leonard Firestone and Troy Robertson, Firestone and Robertson Distilling Company is responsible for giving the world TX Whiskey. F&R released TX Blended Whiskey in June of 2012. TX is a blend of sourced whiskeys, however, in December of 2016, F&R released their TX Straight Bourbon, which is a thoroughly Texas made bourbon... It's badass.

The blended whiskey was awarded "Best American Craft Whiskey" at the 2013 San Francisco World Spirits Competition, and I'm sure the bourbon will end up with similar accolades. Their original location is in Fort Worth in a revitalized pre-Prohibition warehouse just south of downtown. But hold your horses, my friends... this new Whiskey Ranch they built... good gracious, it's amazing.

They bought a country club that overlooks downtown Fort Worth and stuck a $17 million distillery and visitor's center in the middle of the golf course that Ben Hogan and Byron Nelson used to caddy. I KNOW, RIGHT? Glen Gardens Country Club was built in 1912, and F&R is preserving the grounds, and maintaining the golf course, which is only available for friends, family, and the occasional charity events. Whiskey Ranch will be the largest distillery west of the Mississippi River and will also use a 45-foot copper column still in full view of visitors. This is the type of place that will bring whiskey tourism to Fort Worth. Seriously. It's the bees knees.

When discussing the new TX Straight Bourbon, Firestone said, "This is Texas corn, Texas wheat, Texas water, Texas climate, and our Texas yeast." Head distiller, Rob Arnold, gathered samples of yeast from all over North Texas and then took them to TCU for a DNA analysis. They wound up choosing the one from the pecan nut on a friend's ranch... sounds about right.

Both whiskeys are available in Texas and in a growing number of states throughout the United States in most major liquor stores.

TEXAS GENTLEMAN

Firestone & Robertson
901 W Vickery Blvd
Fort Worth, TX 76104
(817) 840-9140
frdistilling.com

This will warm you up with some TX Whiskey and pep you up with Austin's own Caffe Del Fuego. Think of this as a coffee old fashioned.

Glassware: **Rocks Glass**
Garnish: **Orange Peel**

- **2 oz TX blended whiskey**
- **.5 oz Caffe Del Fuego**
- **3 dashes Fee Brothers Aztec Chocolate bitters**

1. Combine whiskey, Caffe Del Fuego, and bitters in a rocks glass over ice.

2. Garnish with an orange peel.

THE FLEUR DU MAL

Paschall Bar
122 N Locust St
Denton, TX 76201

Paschall Bar is cocktail bar in a college town in Denton, TX. I couldn't believe it myself the first time I walked in. Owned collectively by the band Midlake, Paschall Bar is the hippest spot in a town that's known as one of the hippest towns in Texas. The cocktail, named after Charles Baudelaire's volume of poetry—"Les Fleurs du Mal" or "The Flowers of Evil"—is a riff on a Corpse Reviver #2. Elegant, sexy, and inviting, the Fleur du Mal was originally a Valentine feature crafted for the lonely hearts at The Paschall Bar; since then, it's become one of their most beloved and endeared cocktails.

Glassware: **Coupe Glass**
Garnish: **Dried Rose Buds**

- **1 oz gin**
- **1 oz Lillet Blanc**
- **1 oz St. Germain**
- **.5 oz lemon juice**
- **.5 oz grapefruit juice**
- **.25 oz grenadine**
- **.25 oz Kina Tonic**

1. Shake and double strain into a coupe glass.

2. Spritz with orange blossom water.

3. Garnish with dried rose buds.

SOUTHERN SHIPWRECK

Rapscallion
2023 Greenville Ave #110
Dallas, TX 75206
(469) 291-5660
dallasrapscallion.com

Built to be a beautiful addition to the Lower Greenville neighborhood, Rapscallion is one of the best programs in town. As they say, it's "creative, expansive, but not expensive." The Southern Shipwreck has a bit of a tiki vibe to it and the combination of navy strength rum and the slight sweetness of the TX Whiskey makes this drink a bold yet refreshing experience.

Glassware: **Coupe Glass**
Garnish: **Sugar**

- **1 oz Smith and Cross**
- **1 oz TX whiskey**
- **.75 oz lime**
- **.75 oz orgeat**
- **.25 oz brown sugar syrup**
- **5 dashes Scrappys chocolate bitters**

1. Combine ingredients in a shaker with ice and shake vigorously.

2. Strain into a sugar-rimmed coupe glass.

THE GREENVILLE GRANNY

Alamo Club
1919 Greenville Ave
Dallas, Texas 75206
(469) 399-7600
alamoclubdallas.com

Although it opened in 2019, Alamo Club feels as though it's always been a part of Lowest Greenville. This is a collaboration between Austin Rodgers and one of the OG cocktail bartenders in Dallas, Matt Orth. Alamo Club has a fantastic quality food and drinks menu and is a very laid back. For this infusion, make sure you give it a good three to four days before using.

Glassware: **Collins Glass**
Garnish: **Green Apple Slice, Grated Nutmeg**

- **1.5 oz. Tito's Handmade Vodka infused with Granny Smith Apples**
- **.75 oz. Licor 43**
- **.5 oz. fresh lime juice**
- **Fever Tree Ginger Beer, to top**

1. Build the cocktail in the glass, fill with ice, and top with ginger beer.

2. Garnish with slice of apple and grated nutmeg.

—A CONVERSATION WITH—
Michael Martensen

You started at The Mansion in 2007. How was the reception to these drinks?

I had the wealthiest people in Texas walking in and ordering Miller Lite. Did I want to have Miller Lite? No. But the people paying my bills were the people drinking Miller Lite. I had to re-train some people but overall, everyone was 100% all-in. I did get a little bit crazy, midway in when I was feeling it like, "Oh yes, I'm killing it. I'm going to put 10 ingredients to this cocktail now. Look at how great this cocktail is." I was young and stupid. Those cocktails didn't last long.

How did your approach to making drinks change because of being in Texas?

Of course, not being from Texas, we all have a perception of Texas. In my mind, I have three drinks that will always be there... tequila, champagne (because it's a fancy), and I like the idea of using both spice and peach because we're in Texas.

The reception of Dallas to the bar was amazing. People were coming in. It was hot because there were artists. It was like George Michaels was coming in all the time, and all these affluent people of Dallas that are—Not affluent, I mean they're wealthy but they're also artistically affluent.

It's the cool kids with social collateral.

It's the cool kids, and so there's all kinds of stuff going on. The head bartender at The Mansion really is the key to a city. You can make somebody's trip to Dallas so much more if they're open to it, and I love that part about Dallas. I love that it's a big enough city but small enough town to get things done.

So talk to me about The Cedars Social.

I met Brian Williams within about a year and a half of working that job. Then, we decided to open a place together. We opened up in 2011 and I had just spent almost 3 years going to the best bars all across the US, so I had plenty of ideas.

So, I'm familiar with Dallas and The Cedars, at the time, was not in a good neighborhood. Why did you put that thing there?

Jack Mathews gave us free rent for two years. When you know you don't have to pay rent you can open it up and do something special. If you look at the cocktail world, every single influential cocktail bar has been in the ghetto. Milk and Honey, Bourbon & Branch, Tenderloin, Violet Hour... all in bad parts of town.

To you, what is a Texas cocktail?

A Texas cocktail, I've actually thought about this and this is what I do enjoy about Texas drinking and Texas cocktail. We all know East and West Coast are the biggest influencers of the modern American Cocktail, East-West coast, what Texas is to me is the Third Coast. You've got McAllen growing ridiculous citrus and the best grapefruits in the world. Then, you've got this whole whiskey component that Texas has become very good at. You've also got some of the most amazing spirits in the world just south of us. And you tie that up into a Texas atmosphere which is true southern hospitality. And we're influenced by it all. A Texas cocktail is Americana.

~ BLESSING OF AGAVE ~

Shoals Sound and Service
2614 Elm St Ste 110
Dallas, Texas
(972) 808-6976

Shoals is open. It was a long process, full of temporary licenses and hosting pop ups, but it's done, it's here, and Omar Yeefoon and Michael Martensen now run one of the coolest spots in town. Shoals is one of the most-stripped down, straightforward bars they've ever collaborated on. Shoals is classics, done perfectly, no bullshit. Shoals feels like you've found yourself in Omar's living room. He's playing records (his call, not yours) and being the consummate host. It's relaxed and cool and a very easy place to be. You can order whatever you want at Shoals, but the menu is just classic cocktails. I did convince Omar to contribute an original recipe, however. This flip is Texas in a glass.

Glassware: **Coupe Glass**
Garnish: **Grapefruit Peel**

- **1.5 oz Tequila Cabeza**
- **.5 oz aperol**
- **.75 oz fresh grapefruit**
- **.25 oz lime juice**
- **.5 oz agave syrup**
- **Egg white**

1. Combine all ingredients and dry shake without ice for 10 seconds.

2. Shake with ice for 30 seconds.

3. Fine mesh strain into a coupe glass.

4. Garnish with a grapfruit peel.

PANHANDLE WIND

Miss Angeline's
125 E Oak St
Denton, TX 76201
(940) 800-8090
instagram.com/missangelinesdenton

Located in historic downtown Denton on Oak Street, Miss Angeline's is a homestead that has been converted into a cocktail parlor that specializes in cocktails on tap, infusions, craft beer, and mocktails. This has one of the best patios in the state, let alone Denton, and Jeremy Dean has come over from Paschall Bar to make this craft cocktail spot just as stellar. The bar is named after an 1800s Denton bartender nicknamed Miss Angeline, who managed to keep operating when alcohol sales were banned by offering 10-cent peanut specials that came with a free shot of whiskey. The Panhandle Wind is a spicy and refreshing riff on an Aperol gin sour and is perfectly built for patio weather.

Glassware: **Coupe Glass**
Garnish: **Red Bell Pepper Slice**

- **X strawberries**
- **2 tablespoons agave syrup**
- **1 oz gin**
- **.5 oz Aperol**
- **1 oz fresh lemon juice**
- **.25 oz Pepper Tincture**

1. Muddle strawberries in a cocktail shaker with the agave.

2. Add remaining ingredients to the shaker with ice, shake vigorously, and strain into a the glass.

3. Garnish with a red bell pepper slice

—Bar Draught—

BARDRAUGHT.COM

I'd be remiss if I didn't talk about my own company, because I genuinely believe that we're about to change the craft cocktail industry. A few years back, when my favorite cocktail was a "Jim Beam on the rocks," my business partner, Adrian Verdin, and I created and produced a TV pilot about craft cocktails… See, I come from a theatre/film directing background and knew how to tell a story, but didn't know a thing about cocktails. Fast forward to us in LA, at Harvard & Stone, discussing ways we could introduce more people to cocktails by creating an indie music/cocktail festival.

We almost booked The Flaming Lips, we almost booked The Roots, we almost booked Interpol, but nothing seemed to quite work out. But my biggest concern was, "How the hell are we going to serve craft cocktails to 7,000 people anyway?" Adrian told me that he had draft systems at his restaurant and so we started there.

Once we built our first machine, we abandoned the music festival because we could tell the draft cocktail system was the idea we were supposed to run with. Using a combination of our one-of-a kind mobile draft system and our line of all natural, organic mixers, we've created a way for venues to serve craft cocktails in places where it's currently impossible. Ballrooms, stadium concourses, the middle of huge music festivals (see? It all comes full circle), and anywhere that you can't pull off a full cocktail bar. We're damn proud of it and we're damn proud that it was born in Texas. If you ever need to serve a ridiculous amount of cocktails to a ridiculously large group of people, call me.

COSMIC COWBOY COFFEE

Tulips FTW
112 St Louis Ave
Fort Worth, TX 76104
(817) 367-9798
www.tulipsftw.com

If you're looking for the best cocktails in a music venue, Tulips FTW is waiting for you. Owner Jason Suder grew up with some amazing Fort Worth venues that have all disappeared and jumped on the opportunity to fill a void. Born from the need to further establish music as a cultural driver for the city, the idea was always to have the best sound, the best bands, and, most importantly, the best bar program at any venue in the state. Matthew Harber, CEO of Spune Productions, has done an amazing job of convincing national acts to spend their North Texas dates in Fort Worth instead of Dallas and the community is thriving around this new approach to its music scene. But you're here for the cocktails, so I present you with Torry Cray's CBD-laced riff on an espresso martini!

Glassware: Coupe Glass
Garnish: Coffee Beans

- **1.5 oz Balcones Pot Still Texas Bourbon**
- **1 oz espresso shot (ideally made Fort Worth Single-Origin Counter Culture Coffee)**
- **.75 oz vanilla bean demerara syrup**
- **.25 ml Martha Stewart Unflavored CBD oil (optional)**

1. Combine all ingredients in a cocktail shaker with ice, shake vigorously, and strain into glass.

2. Garnish with two coffee beans

—The Mansion—

2821 TURTLE CREEK BLVD
DALLAS, TX 75219
(214) 443-4747
ROSEWOODHOTELS.COM/EN/MANSION-ON-TURTLE-CREEK-DALLAS/DINING/MANSION-RESTAURANT

When The Rosewood Mansion was renovated in 2007, it brought with it somewhat of a revolution in the Dallas culinary scene. John Tesar (of Kitchen Confidential fame) took over the reins from Dallas' culinary darling, Dean Fearing. He quickly elevated The Mansion to iconic status, earning one of the only 5 star reviews in Dallas' history. Of course, he also became known as "Dallas' Most Hated Chef," but for our purposes he's a hero. John believes that a bar program is essential to greatness, and when he took over the joint, he brought with him the arrival of Michael Martensen.

SHRUB YOU THE RIGHT WAY

This was, arguably, the first craft cocktail program in the state, but it was certainly a place that changed cocktails in Texas forever. The great Danny Caffall has been running the bar program for quite a while and this cocktail is a great example of complex flavors while still maintaining approachability.

Glassware: **Rocks Glass**
Garnish: **Lemon Twist**

- **2 oz Maker's Mark bourbon**
- **.75 oz peach shrub**
- **.5 oz fresh lemon juice**
- **.5 oz creme de noyaux**
- **1 dash peach bitters**

1. Mix all ingredients in shaker tin.

2. Shake and pour.

3. Garnish with mint. You may also top with ginger beer to add a little frizante.

Peach Shrub

Combine peach puree, sugar, and sherry vinegar.

RUBY TWILITE

Twilite Lounge
2640 Elm St
Dallas, TX 75226
(214) 741-2121
thetwilitelounge.com

Twilite Lounge is one of my favorite bars in Dallas. Started by two musicians, Danny Balis (Calhoun among other things) and Jess Barr (Slobberbone among other things), Twilite is their version of a New Orleans style neighborhood venue, where on occasion a great blues man or singer-songwriter would pop in for a few tunes. They have a killer frozen Irish Coffee that they would not let me use for the book because they were sworn to secrecy by the New Orleans bar that gave it to them. Head Bartender Andrew Thompson recognizes that it's a shot-and-a-beer type place, but will occasionally talk some folks into trying something new... Like putting beer on top of your vodka cocktail.

Glassware: **Highball Glass**
Garnish: **Grapefruit Wedge**

- **1 oz Deep Eddy Ruby Grapefruit vodka**
- **4 oz lemonade**
- **Topped off with a float of Shiner Ruby Redbird beer**

Layer all ingredients in a glass with the beer going last. Made to give the appearance of a Texas sunset.

—A CONVERSATION WITH—
Brad Hensarling

How did you end up at The Chat Room?

I started dating a gal, who lived down the street. We got to know the owner, John, who's now my business partner. In 2006, he sold the bar but bought it back and he wanted me to come in 50/50 in order to basically remove his old business partner.

That led to your cocktail education?

Well, when I was still doing the chain restaurants, I had a few people ask for a Manhattan or an Old Fashioned and I did the best I could… but I didn't know any recipes. I couldn't google anything. I just knew there was whiskey and vermouth in it and I used the only vermouth we had, which was probably six months old and left on the back bar. I wanted to be the best I could be if this was going to be my job and I tried the Manhattan that I had made and it was bad.

So what was your solution?

Simple art of self-evaluation… and boredom at the Chat Room. If I was going to be in business for myself, then maybe I should do it well. I picked up *The Joy of Mixology*. And I had hours upon hours to practice. We're talking six to seven hours a day, I was doing nothing else. I came in at 4, we got busy at 11:30. I had plenty of time to teach myself. I remember getting to a point in the book where Regan starts showing how to make these recipe trees and these templates for his cocktails. So I took that simple idea and started experimenting.

So how did you end up deciding that opening up a cocktail bar in Fort Worth, Texas in 2009 was a good idea?

So, there was a girl who really hated the Chat Room, but always came to the Chat Room. One day, she came in and said "I'm gonna open a bar across the street and take all your customers." So I went to my landlord and said "Here's a check for the deposit when it comes up for lease."

So it's 2009, you and I both know that Fort Worth is a whiskey & Coke and beer scene; how was the reception?

Well, no one knew what a cocktail was. For better or worse, we decided not to carry a lot of things. We couldn't do a 7&7 for instance. People around me always preferred a good product, but what I was able to serve them (at the Chat Room) was always subpar. I wanted to fix that.

People started coming to The Usual and started getting great drinks and then they'd go on with their evening. So I'd start getting calls from bartenders at restaurants around town saying "Hey man... what's in this?" I was always liberal with the recipes, but I was always thinking "Dude, you don't have velvet falernum. You can't make it anyway."

And now we have cocktails man! That's it. I'm the one that fell on the sword for it, obviously I'm not the only one, but in this area, in this town... somebody had to at some point. I just decided to be the chump. But it's worked out alright.

—The Usual—

1408 W Magnolia Ave
Fort Worth, Texas
(817) 810-0114

The Usual was the first cocktail-focused bar that opened in North Texas. It would be years after it's opening (in 2009) before anyone in the entire metroplex would try to open anything specifically driven by cocktails.

The Usual is my favorite bar in Texas. I know I'm not supposed to play favorites, but it's been my favorite bar in Texas for damn near ten years now. The Usual, to me, is the perfect balance between innovation and creativity and the relaxed, welcoming, the feeling you get when you've entered your neighborhood dive bar. The program at The Usual singlehandedly dragged Fort Worth, Texas into the cocktail scene. Now if you're opening up a restaurant in Fort Worth, you have to have some sort of cocktail menu. The city expects it, and odds are your first classic cocktail was an Old Fashioned at The Usual.

AMBASSADOR PUNSCH

About the Ambassador Punsch, Brad told me, "No one orders this drink until they try it, but when they do they're hooked." Swedish Punsch used to be an incredibly important part of many cocktails, but disappeared because of Prohibition.

Glassware: **Coupe Glass**
Garnish: **Lime Wheel**

- **1 oz Zaya rum**
- **1 oz Kronan Swedish Punsch**
- **.5 oz rich simple syrup**
- **.5 oz lime juice**
- **6 drops Elemakule Tiki bitters**

1. Combine ingredients in a shaker with ice and shake vigorously.

2. Strain into a coupe glass.

3. Garnish with a lime wheel.

PEACHY KEANE

Ida Claire
5001 Belt Line Rd
Dallas, TX 75254
(214) 377-8227
ida-claire.com

Ida Claire is built on Southern hospitality. From the same group that created Whiskey Cake and Mexican Sugar, Ida Claire is all about the Southern kitsch. And when you think Southern, you think peaches. This cocktail is named for Margaret D. H. Keane (b. 1927) who was an American artist who mainly painted women, children, and animals, most notably with big eyes. She sold works under her husband's name for years and only received credit after divorcing him.

Glassware: **Rocks Glass**
Garnish: **Dried Peach, Ginger Candy**

- **1 oz Old Forester bourbon**
- **.5 oz Giffard Peche de Vigne**
- **.5 oz King's Ginger Liqueur**
- **.75 oz honey**
- **.75 oz lemon juice**
- **Egg white**

1. Combine all ingredients and dry shake without ice for 10 seconds.
2. Shake with ice for 30 seconds.
3. Fine strain into a rocks glass.
4. Garnish with a dried peach and ginger candy.

LIPSTICK & ROUGE

Pie 3.14
2560 King Arthur Blvd #100
Lewisville, TX 75056
(972) 899-2718
pie314everydayeatery.com

Sean Conner is old-school Dallas. The man originally behind the programs at Whiskey Cake and Mexican Sugar left to live that suburban cocktail life when Pie 3.14 was created. He is now in the midst of a series of projects, all in the suburbs of Dallas, Sean is bringing craft cocktail culture to a different demographic than most. Sometimes it's a pizza joint, sometimes it's a taqueria, but it's always serving killer cocktails. The Lipstick & Rouge is what you want on the patio at about 4:45 in the afternoon... once you've dropped all your kids off at soccer and piano lessons.

Glassware: **Champagne Flute**
Garnish: **Lemon Twist**

- **.75 oz Aperol**
- **.75 oz Luxardo amaretto**
- **.75 oz lemon juice**
- **3 oz prosecco**

1. Combine ingredients in a shaker with ice and shake vigorously.

2. Strain into a champagne flute.

3. Top with Prosecco and garnish with a lemon twist.

LITTLE RYE LIES

Whiskey Cake
3601 Dallas Pkwy
Plano, TX 75093
(972) 993-2253
whiskey-cake.com

Whiskey Cake is singlehandedly changing the suburban cocktail landscape in Texas. With locations outside of Dallas, Houston, and San Antonio, they not only serve classic cocktails with the precision of their urban counterparts, but they also host classes and happy hours specifically to educate their guests.

Glassware: **Rocks Glass**
Garnish: **Mint, Orange Peel**

- **2 oz Old Overholt rye whiskey**
- **.5 oz black tea infused simple syrup**
- **2 dashes Reagan's orange bitters**
- **1 dash of Angostura bitters**

1. Stir all ingredients with rocks ice and strain over a large rock.

2. Garnish with fresh mint and orange peel.

KNOB CREEK
KNOB CREEK RYE
GENTLEMAN JACK
nitro

SAN ANTONIO

"I THINK TEXANS HAVE MORE FUN THAN THE REST OF THE WORLD."

—Tommy Tune

It's not just the cocktail conference that makes San Antonio one of the most exciting cocktail scenes in the United States, but it certainly helps. Once a year, San Antonio gets to show off to all of those attending the largest cocktail event in Texas. But San Antonio's cocktail history was sparked by the conference's founder, Sasha Petraske.

Sasha became part of the San Antonio community and his training methods and approach changed the city's culinary scene forever. There are those who do not come directly from Sasha's tutelage, but every single cocktail bar that has opened in San Antonio has benefited by Sasha's presence. Combine world-class training and pedigree with the enormous impact of Mexican culture on the city as a whole, and San Antonio has a different vibe than anywhere in the world.

THUNDER GUN EXPRESS

Blue Box
312 Pearl Pkwy #2107
San Antonio, TX 78215
(210) 227-2583
blueboxbar.com

Blue Box Bar is located in the historic Pearl district in San Antonio. Back in the day when the brewery was up and running, employees were allowed to drink on the job. During the day, employees would pull beer from the line to consume, but it was always monitored by the foreman. So the overnight workers, in order to make sure they had the same drinking privileges as their daytime counterparts, kept their beer in an unmarked blue cooler, or the "Blue Box." The Pearl Brewery is no longer operational, but the area has become a haven for incredible food and drinks.

Glassware: **Rocks Glass**

- **4 orange wedges**
- **2 dashes cardamon bitters**
- **.75 oz TX honey syrup 1:1 water honey (TX wildflower honey)**
- **.75 oz amaro Montenegro**
- **1 oz mezcal vida**

1. Muddle oranges.

2. Add remaining ingredients plus ice and shake vigorously.

3. Strain into a rocks glass.

KILL GIL

Bohanon's
219 E Houston St
San Antonio, TX 78205
(210) 472-2600
bohanans.com

Bohanan's has one of the most important cocktail programs in Texas. By hiring Sasha Petraske (Milk & Honey, The Varnish) they started the cocktail scene in San Antonio. Sasha was hired to revamp the Bohanan's cocktail program in 2010 Texas cocktails have never been the same. With a vision built around education and apprenticeship, the amount of scene-changing bartenders who have come out Bohanan's (and then gone on to train their own crews) is absolutely staggering. If there was a Mount Rushmore of Texas Cocktails, Sasha Petraske would be on it. He's an honorary Texan.

Glassware: **Rocks Glass**
Garnish: **Orange Zest**

- **2 oz Gentleman Jack**
- **.25 oz Benedictine**
- **.75 oz Tempus Fugit Gran Classico**

1. Stir all ingredients and serve over a large rock.

2. Zest an orange as garnish.

—A CONVERSATION WITH —
Jeret Pena

When did cocktails start making sense to you?

I didn't really understand cocktails until I went to go see Bobby Heugel at the Anvil. Three weeks after he opened I went to go see Bobby, and I started watching him make cocktails.

Then Sasha came along. I was working at the bar that all these guys would come drink at after their shifts learning from Sasha. That dove-tailed beautifully because, while I was learning all of these interesting, cool new style[s] of cocktails, I started learning the craft of making traditional, classic cocktails and the technique behind it. It was really interesting, the timing. I was learning technique through Timmy Bryand and Chris Ware.

Then from there, David Allen, my buddy, started talking to Chris Hill, who owns the Esquire Tavern and introduced us and on December 26th in 2010. He offered me the job to run Esquire, the bar program.

Let's chat about the James Beard Award.

Okay... so this starts with Jason Dady telling me that starchefs.com was coming. I looked them up and I realized that, "Oh, no Bobby is in here, Eric Castro is in here. Jason Litrell." So I called Bobby, and asked him what to expect.

And he was like, "Hey, just give them the four best drinks that represents who you are." So, for months, I was just kind of just wracking my brain like, "What am I going to serve the people?" It turns out I served them four really good drinks.

So cocktail conference comes around and I got a call telling me I won the starchef for the rising star. I put it on mute and was screaming at the top of my lungs.

I usually turn off my ringer, but I got a call at 8:00 in the morning, the day of the gala. My friend, Jennifer McInnis told me I got a James Beard nomination. I was hungover and dehydrated, and emotional. I started crying. I was like, "This is hilarious."

So what does the scene look like now?

Looking at the industry as a whole, I've come to realize that we won, the cocktail movement won. That it's no longer a fad because everyone is doing it. You have places on the Riverwalk that are serving Moscow Mules versus five years ago when that wasn't a thing. Now, we are just a victim of our own success. Now, everyone is doing it, like it's almost kind of lost its allure somewhat.

You can't just be a cocktail bar anymore. I personally think Stay Golden is a good start concept to get—It's a test market. We are testing the market right now. We're creating basically dive craft cocktail bars.

NOCHES DE AMOR

Amor Eterno
540 S Presa St
San Antonio, TX 78205
instagram.com/amoreterno_sa

One of the newest offerings from San Antonio bar pros, Brian Correa and Aaron Peña, Amor Eterno is in the heart of Southtown, just behind the iconic Bar America. Amor Eterno is a beautiful and super hip lounge where you can enjoy a brilliant cocktail and have an intimate conversation. Fun fact, Peña's Noches De Amor is named after a cumbia he randomly heard at an airport in Memphis, Tennessee. He says this cocktail is "something easy, something sexy, just like the bar itself."

Glassware: **Coupe Glass**
Garnish: **Dehydrated Strawberries**

- **1.5 oz blanco tequila**
- **1 oz Strawberry Syrup**
- **.5 oz fresh lime juice**
- **Champagne, to top**

1. Combine all ingredients, except the Champagne, in a cocktail shaker filled with ice, shake vigorously, and strain into a chilled glass.

2. Top with Champagne and garnish with dehydrated strawberries.

Strawberry Syrup

- 1 cup fresh cut strawberries
- 1 cup water
- 1 cup sugar

1. Combine all ingredients in a saucepan over medium-high heat, bring to a boil, and stir to dissolve all of the sugar.
2. Let cool, strain, and store in refrigerator up to 1 month.

—Ranger Creek—

TJ, Dennis, and Mark met coming out of business school while working for the same San Antonio corporation. They quickly realized that they were three guys with a passion for beer, whiskey, entrepreneurship, and, most importantly, a growing discontent for corporate life. They literally couldn't decide if they were leaning more towards a brewery or a distillery, so they made both. I mean, how hard could opening up a distillery be? (It's hard. It's incredibly hard. I dare say, kids, don't try this at home…)

Ranger Creek is a combined brewery/distillery located in San Antonio. As a combined operation, they can do things to highlight the relationship between beer and whiskey that not many others can. So much of the equipment is the same to make both beer and whiskey, and there are a lot of similarities between the two processes. They can age their own beer in their own bourbon barrels and distill their beers into whiskeys.

One of the coolest programs they have is their white dog barrel experiment they've been working on for seven years. I've heard of distillers working with small barrels… I've heard of distillers loving them, hating them, and everything in between, but I've never heard of anyone giving the public the opportunity the chance to try the experiment themselves.

Here's how it works, they take their white dog whiskey and they age it in nontraditional small barrels (5 gallons and 10 gallons) and get mature whiskey in about a year. Simultaneously, they age the same white dog whiskey in traditional large barrels (which obviously takes longer) and then do a tasting where you can try the same exact white dog in small and large barrels and do a direct comparison. Mark McDavid, one of the founders of Ranger Creek, said, "No one's ever actually released the results of these experiments, it's just been distillers tasting them behind closed doors. We wanted to present it to the public to try them blind and side by side and they can see what they like better. You have to be kind of nerdy to appreciate it, haha!"

Sidenote: Ranger Creek is also a kickstarter success story. They used the crowdfunding platform to fund their inaugural release of their OPA six packs on the brewery side.

RANGER CREEK TEA TAPPER

Ranger Creek
Recipe: Dani Call

Nothing like a Texas sweet tea... it can only be improved with some great Texas whiskey.

Glassware: **Rocks Glass**
Garnish: **Orange and Lemon Slices**

- **2 oz sweet tea**
- **.75 oz pomegranate juice**
- **1.5 oz Ranger Creek .36 Texas bourbon**
- **1 slice lemon**
- **1 slice orange**

1. Fill a rocks glass with ice, add ingredients, and stir.

2. Mix liquids in and stir.

3. Rim glass with lemon. Garnish with orange and lemon slices.

Hint: Scale the recipe up to pitcher-size by multiplying all the liquid quantities by 5.

LE PETIT PRINCE

Pastiche
1506 E Houston St
San Antonio, TX 78202
(540) 305-4506
facebook.com/pastiche.sa/

Pastiche is a Moulin Rouge throwback-style bar with a cool, French art nouveau vibe. Focusing on French classics, owners Benjamin Krick and Lucas Bradbury have created a unique experience in the place where the margaritas are from. This cocktail, named by Krick after the French story The Little Prince, is herbal and full bodied with a crisp minerality that brings forth flavors of orange blossom, nectar, and fresh thyme.

Glassware: **Nick & Nora Glass**
Garnish: **Thyme**

- **1.5 oz Citadelle Gin**
- **1 oz Sauternes**
- **.5 oz Lillet Blanc**
- **1 barspoon Bigallet Thyme Liqueur**
- **2 dashes Regans Orange Bitters**

1. Combine all ingredients in a cocktail shaker with ice, shake vigorously, and strain into the glass.

2. Garnish with a sprig of thyme.

Jasper's Basic Stock

- 6 oz lime juice
- .5 cup piloncillo sugar
- .75 oz Angostura Bitters
- Half a nutmeg, freshly grated

1. Combine lime juice and sugar a mason jar and stir to dissolve the sugar.

2. Add the remaining ingredients, put the lid on the mason jar, and shake well until it's completely combined and liquified. Refrigerate for up to 1 month.

BERTA'S CUP

Jet-Setter
229 E Houston St #10
San Antonio, TX 78205
(540) 305-4506
jet-settersa.com/

Jet-Setter rose from the ashes of Juniper Tar, one of the best, now gone, cocktail bars in Texas. This incredibly approachable cocktail is Benjamin Krick's cross between a Moscow mule and a Pimms Cup, using tropical flavors from Mexico. The cocktail is named after Berta Zerón de García, the first woman in Mexico to pilot a jet, participate in international air races, and become a skydiver.

Glassware: **Mexican Clay Mug**
Garnish: **Cucumber Ribbon**

- **1.5 oz Charanda Rum**
- **1 oz Jasper's Basic Stock**
- **.5 oz fresh cucumber juice**
- **.5 oz passion fruit syrup**
- **Goya Ginger Beer, to top**

1. Combine all ingredients in a cocktail shaker with ice, shake vigorously, and strain into the mug over ice.

2. Top with ginger beer and garnish with a cucumber ribbon.

—Esquire Tavern—

155 E COMMERCE ST
SAN ANTONIO, TX 78205
(210) 222-2521
ESQUIRETAVERN-SA.COM

The Esquire Tavern is San Antonio history. The door originally opened on Repeal Day in 1933. San Antonio's oldest bar went through a massive makeover in 2011. Its vintage décor, classic furnishings, and dusky lighting which creates an intimate, yet lively atmosphere. This is the only Riverwalk bar you need to go to in San Antonio, trust me.

There's one in every city… one bar that is quintessentially the centerpiece of their entire scene. The Esquire Tavern is that for San Antonio. Maybe it's the James Beard nominations for best bar program (they have two) or maybe it's the pedigree of those who have been a part of the program and moved on to other amazing projects, but it's certainly one of the most respected and revered bars in all of Texas. Houston Eaves is now leading the bar program, and you can see his agave centric roots all over the menu.

LA TIERRA DE VIEJITAS

Recipe: Houston Eaves, Myles Worrell, & Hank Cathey, Downstairs, 2016

I'm frankly thrilled to present La Tierra De Viejitas, namely because I've wanted this recipe from the moment I saw it on a menu.

Glassware: **Beer Glass**
Garnish: **Nutmeg**

- **1.5 oz Lustau Brandy de Jerez Solera Gran Reserva**
- **.75 oz Café du Monde Chicory Cold Brew**
- **.5 oz Cardamaro**
- **1 oz Henriques & Henriques Rainwater Madeira-Coconut Cream**

1. Add madeira-coconut cream to bottom of chilled, tulip-shaped beer glass, and add crushed ice to fill glass.

2. Combine other ingredients in mixing tin, and then pour on top of cream and crushed ice.

3. Garnish with freshly grated nutmeg.

¡SIN MAÍZ NO HAY PAÍS!

Esquire Tavern Downstairs
Recipe: Houston Eaves, Myles Worrell, & Hank Cathey, Downstairs, 2016
155 E Commerce St
San Antonio, TX 78205
(210) 222-2521

Okay, so... here's a little secret... there's a speakeasy inside a cocktail bar in San Antonio. Meta, I know. But the Downstairs at Esquire Tavern is truly a different world than the raucous party happening above. With Hank Cathey coming up with some of the most innovative drinks and drink presentations in the city, Downstairs is an experience in and of its own. With an entrance on the Riverwalk itself, Downstairs is an intimate lounge dishing out "unconventional inclinations." This place is nice. I'm talking really nice. This isn't a cocktail dive bar... this is, unapologetically, the nicest bar on the Riverwalk and the drinks are absolutely incredible. This big batch recipe will make you look like a rockstar party host.

Glassware: **Rocks Glass**
Garnish: **Mint Sprig, Nutmeg**

- **4 qts Jamaican rum (Hamilton Jamaican gold)**
- **1 qt lime juice**
- **3 qts pineapple juice**
- **2 qts orange juice**
- **1 qt sherry (1:1:1 Fino:Oloroso:Palo Cortado)**
- **4 qts whole milk**
- **16 oz coconut cream**
- **32 oz corn**

1. Combine rum, lime juice, pineapple juice, orange juice, and sherry to create a juice mix.

2. In a large pot, combine whole milk, coconut cream, and corn. Heat until boiling. Strain corn. Slowly add liquid to juice mix.

3. Strain through a super bag slowly. Continue to strain mixture no less than three times, changing out the catch container but not the super bag, after each strain has run through.

4. The more you strain, the more clear the punch will be. Each passing through will take longer than the last. Do not agitate the bag in any way while straining.

5. Bottle and chill.

6. Serve individually over large piece of ice in a rocks glass, and garnish with mint sprig and grated nutmeg. Enjoy!

—A CONVERSATION WITH—
Cathy Siegel

When did the San Antonio Cocktail Conference begin?

Well, the first cocktail conference was held in January of 2012.

Were you there?

Yes, when I participated the first year, that was because I was the Executive Director of the original beneficiary agency from the cocktail conference.

So, how was it? What was it like?

A bunch of people who are all friends joined hands and jumped off the edge of the cliff and they never looked down to see if there was water. They were just confident that if they held hands and they were all friends and they believed in each other and they believed in the cause that everything would be fine. It was. They didn't have some great master plan and the blueprints for a successful event. They just believed in the cause and in each other.

What was the cause?

The original beneficiary agency. We were giving money to help bring children to San Antonio from all over the world, from developing countries, who needed our help to get repaired with heart surgery. It felt good to be doing it for charity, and to be doing good in Texas. From the beginning, participating industry people from out of town would say it felt like doing a festival in your neighborhood.

Even as we've grown, I think we maintained that feeling with people. We issued almost 10,000 tickets in 2017. We have people coming from all over the world and yet it still feels like a neighborhood event.

So how has the growth of the conference impacted San Antonio?

I think it feels really good to the food and beverage community to do this event together to benefit children's causes. And it feels really good to show off our city and our talents this way.

I would tell you that the growth of the cocktail scene in San Antonio, if you look at the number of true craft cocktail bars in the city in 2011 until now, the growth of the number of places and the growth of the cocktail conference, my guess would be similar.

Same question but for Texas.

I think it's the exact same thing. I think its growth matches our own growth. I think it felt good to bring this to people down to Texas. Texans are a funny breed and we are very, very vocal about our pride in being from or living in Texas.

In Texas we are Texans. I am proud of people coming to San Antonio to experience the San Antonio cocktail conference. I think we as Texans are proud that this massive amount of people are coming to Texas to celebrate craft cocktails.

What are other differentiators between SACC and other cocktail events across the country?

First and foremost, the charity component. That ... 100% of our profits go to support children's charities. That makes it different right off the bat. Also we have much more involvement from the consumer in our festival than in any other festival I can think of. We are creating more competent consumers. That's really wonderful.

What's on the docket for the future of SACC?

I hope that the future of SACC is such that more and more people will want to invest their time, energy, and dollars in the product so that we can begin to grow our contribution to children's care. I hope that we will continue to reach more and more people throughout the United States so that we can continue to grow this community of people that enjoy craft cocktails together. We intend to be around for a long time, but as we grow what I hope is that we are always approachable.

KAMEHAMEHA

Hot Joy
1014 S Alamo St
San Antonio, TX 78210
(210) 368-9324
hotjoysa.com

First and foremost, I've been trying to avoid talking about anything that's not cocktail related, but I have to divert for a second. IF you ever find yourself in San Antonio and you are in desperate need for ramen… Go. To. Hot. Joy. There's a reason it was on Bon Appetit's Top 10 list the year it opened. You'll thank me for this. Hot Joy's always had a killer cocktail program with some of San Antonio's top talent passing through. The Kamehameha is named after the founder and first ruler of Hawaii. It also happens to be a signature move of Goku, the hero of Dragonball Z. So, you see, it has Japanese whisky blended with American whiskey. Get it?

Glassware: **Rocks Glass**
Garnish: **Lemon Twist**

- **1 oz Suntory Toki Japanese whisky**
- **.5 oz Takara Shochu**
- **.5 oz Rittenhouse rye**
- **.5 oz Punt e Mes**
- **2 dashes Angostura bitters**

1. Add all ingredients to a rocks glass with one large ice cube.

2. Garnish with a lemon twist and a smile.

true

THE RATTLE AND THE RHYTHM

Jazz, TX
Recipe: Jake Corney
312 Pearl Parkway, Bld. #6 Suite #6001
San Antonio, TX 78215
(210) 332-9386
jazztx.com

Jazz, TX is a 3,500-square-foot live music venue in a basement in the Pearl District in San Antonio. A Sasha Petraske disciple Jake Corney (formerly at Bohanan's) has crafted a magnificent menu based on the live music vibes ranging from jazz to honky tonk to blues. It's one of the more approachable, yet creative menus in San Antonio, and this cocktail is incredibly refreshing and dangerously easy to drink.

Glassware: **Rocks Glass**
Garnish: **Mint**

- **1.5 oz white rum**
- **.75 oz lime juice**
- **.75 oz simple syrup**
- **.75 oz Jicama Juice**
- **3–4 mint leaves**
- **1 pinch smoked sea salt**
- **2 dashes coffee bitters**

1. Shake all ingredients and strain into a rocks glass.

2. Garnish with mint to serve.

SOMETHING CITRUS-Y, WITH WHISKEY, BOOZE FORWARD

The Modernist
516 E Grayson St
San Antonio, TX 78215
(210) 901-8646
facebook.com/themodernistsa

The Modernist is a laidback mid-century modern-style bar with no menu. Instead, patrons tell the staff what they're in the mood for and then the magic begins. Every cocktail made here is either a classic or a once in a lifetime experience. One can imagine walking in to order "something citrus-y, with whiskey that's booze forward" and thus, you have this gem, David Naylor's riff on the Monte Carlo.

Glassware: **Rocks Glass**
Garnish: **Grapefruit Slice**

- **2 oz Weller Special Reserve**
- **.5 oz Giffard Pamplemousse**
- **2 dashes Angostura Bitters**
- **1 dash Peychaud's Bitters**
- **2 dashes Acid Solution**

1. Combine all ingredients in the rocks glass, add ice, stir until chilled, and top with more ice.

2. Garnish with a grapefruit slice

Acid Solution

- 100 g water
- 20 g citric acid powder
- 10 g malic acid powder

1. In a small bowl, combine all ingredients and stir until powders dissolve; will keep indefinitely in a sealed bottle.

WITHOUT A TRACE

Bar 1919
1420 S Alamo St
San Antonio, TX 78204
(210) 227-1420
bar1919.com

Don Marsh was doing classic cocktails in San Antonio before San Antonio had the foggiest clue what classic cocktails that weren't named "margarita" were. Don's influence is felt all over the city, but Bar 1919 ... that's his bar.. It's the bar Don's always wanted, where he can do whatever he wants. The man has over 600 whiskeys, for crying out loud... Bar 1919 is a dark den of possibilities. You have the best selection of whiskeys in Texas, agave only rivaled by certain mezcalarias, and a cocktail menu as good as any in the state. It's a perfect place to explore new spirits and let Don tell you stories about the old days of San Antonio, but don't get him started in on ice density or you may need another drink.

Glassware: **Old Fashioned Glass**
Garnish: **Orange Peel**

- **1.5 oz Buffalo Trace bourbon**
- **.5 oz Amaro Nonino**
- **.5 oz honey syrup**
- **.5 oz fresh lemon juice**

1. Add all ingredients into a mixing glass and stir.

2. Lace an old fashioned glass with absinthe and lightly drop a large format cube in the glass.

3. Pourand garnish with an orange peel.

—Azar Distilling—

At about 8:15 AM on October 24th, 2014, there was an explosion at Azar Distilling, strong enough to send a man flying through (yes—through) a wall. A small fire was started and it took Bexar County firefighters about 40 minutes to put out the flames. The worker was sent to the hospital, but sustained no injuries… but now he has a hell of a story.

When he arrived on the scene, Trey Azar feared he'd lost everything. To lighten the mood, the volunteer firefighters suggested that he rename the brand "Cinco Fuego." Through sheer force of will, they re-opened just 95 days after the blast.

Proudly hailing from San Antonio, Trey and Kimberly Azar started Azar Distiling in 2010 named after (kinda) their five children. Trey's family has always been in the booze business. His grandfather was the first ever distributor of Coors in Texas, but his family sold off their chain of liquor stores some time ago. The oil and gas industry just wasn't cutting it for him, so Trey and wife Kim decided to jump back on the wagon by designing a premium American vodka, which has won multiple awards in international competitions.

Fast forward to today and here comes Seersucker Gin. Trey said, "We worked for more than a year to accomplish the perfect taste profile that is light on the palate and has recognizable Southern flavors, yet still maintains the nuances that a gin drinker appreciates." Utilizing the same pot distillation as Cinco Vodka, Seersucker is a slick designed, citrus forward gin with notes of honeysuckle and mint to compliment the juniper.

Azar Distilling is in the process of expanding, not just the scope of the brands, but the distillery itself. Cinco Vodka and Seersucker Gin are now available at most major liquor stores throughout Texas, Tennessee, Arkansas, Massachusetts, Oklahoma, and Rhode Island.

SEERSUCKER 75

Azar Distilling
8501 Cover Rd
San Antonio, TX 78263
(210) 648-1500
cincovodka.com

This is a French 75, made with Seersucker gin. This is a recipe you should commit to memory.

Glassware: **Champagne Glass**
Garnish: **Lemon Twist**

- **1 oz Seersucker gin**
- **.5 oz lemon juice**
- **.5 oz simple syrup**
- **Prosecco or champagne**

1. Combine ingredients in a shaker with ice and shake vigorously.

2. Strain into a champagne glass.

3. Top with chilled prosecco or champagne.

4. Garnish with a lemon twist.

The WIDE WORLD of Texas

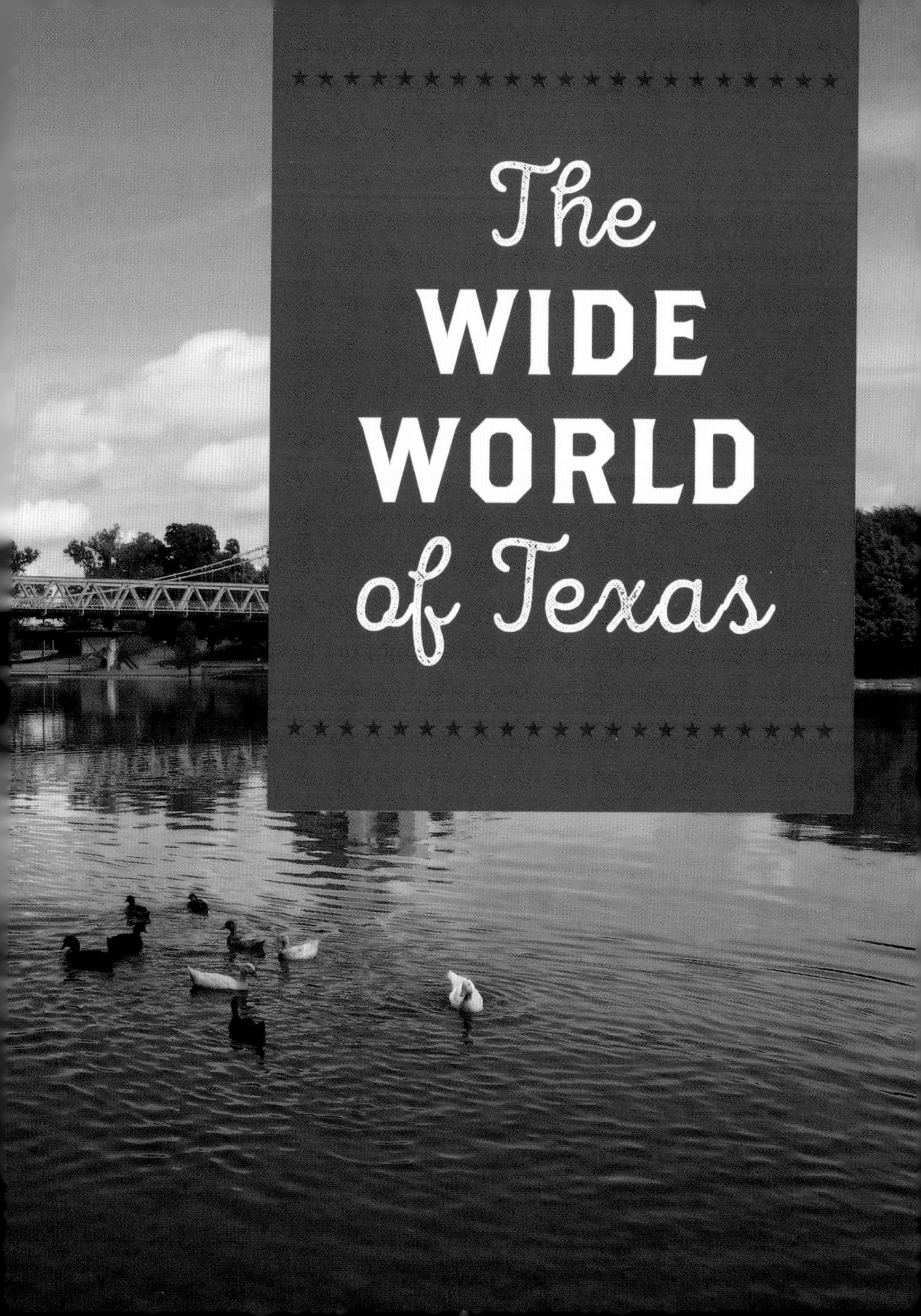

"TEXAS IS NEITHER SOUTHERN NOR WESTERN.
TEXAS IS TEXAS."

—Senator William Blakley

The population of Marfa is 1981, and I have a recipe for you from there. The population of Boerne is 10,471 and I have a recipe for you from there. The population of Texarkana is 34,782 and I have a recipe for you from there.

I think you get the point. When I started this project, I kept picturing a map of Texas. The first thing I said to myself was "You can't just have Dallas, Austin, Houston, and San Antonio." I went into this blindly hoping that the cocktail movement had made it to the hinterlands. Y'all… it has. From McAllen to Amarillo and El Paso to Texarkana, the map's filling itself out nicely. The fact that Waco has gone, in my mind, from that place where they won't let you dance (listen, there were lots of rumors about the Baptists running Baylor) to one of the most important whiskey cities in the world, let alone Texas, is no small feat itself.

Texas is massive. This chapter is the reason I wanted to present this book in this manner. Cocktails are everywhere and I have the map to prove it. While this movement may have started in the city centers, it's the suburbs and the college towns that are coming in to their own. If you can have a cocktail bar in the shadow of Kyle Field be one of the most happening spots in College Station, the world's changed, y'all.

Rosemary Simple Syrup

- 1 cup water
- 8 oz by weight sugar

SMOKEY THE PEAR

Black Pearl
108 W Erwin St
Tyler, TX 75702
(903) 531-2415

It takes some courage to throw cocktails on a menu in Tyler, Texas, but if you're going to do it, you might as well be exceptional at it. Lead by Mitch Murray, Black Pearl serves stellar original and classic cocktails. Their cocktail is based on an unfortunately underused Texas product, the mighty pear. Texas pears are pretty amazing and, often, more available than one might think. In fact, every now and then you'll see pears on abandoned farm sites that are over 100 years old. This is a great combination of the freshness of the pears and the smoke from the rosemary with an underbelly of some magnificent TX whiskey.

Glassware: **Rocks Glass**
Garnish: **Rosemary Sprig**

- **2 oz TX Blended Whiskey**
- **.75 oz Grand Marnier**
- **1 oz lemon juice**
- **.5 oz rosemary simple syrup**
- **¼ of a pear**

1. Add pear, lemon juice, and simple syrup to shaker tin.

2. Muddle the pear, and add remaining ingredients.

3. Shake and fine strain into a rosemary-smoked rocks glass over a large ice cube.

4. Garnish with a fresh rosemary sprig.

RUMBLE OF THE GODS

Dichotomy Coffee & Spirits
508 Austin Ave
Waco, TX 76701
dichotomycs.com

If I was to have you guess what the whiskey capital of Texas was, how many of you would have said Waco? Balcones is one of the most important whiskey producers in the United States, let alone Texas. Rumble is a particularly interesting spirit. Originally built on a dessert sauce template, Rumble isn't a whiskey, nor is it a mead... is it an eau de vie? Maybe? Regardless, it's become a Texas staple and that's why you'll see it all over Dichotomy's menu in Waco, Texas. Dichotomy is half cocktail bar, half coffee shop and they've brought true cocktail culture to Waco, which is quite impressive.

Glassware: **Nick & Nora**
Garnish: **Orange Rind, Maraschino Cherry**

- **1.5 oz rumble**
- **.75 oz orange liqueur**
- **.75 oz lime juice**
- **.25 oz simple syrup**

1. Shake all ingredients and double strain into glass.

2. Garnish with orange rind and maraschino cherry.

—Balcones Distilling—

We're blessed here in the great state of Texas with some incredible terroir, an incredible climate, and some damn creative Texans. Balcones makes some of the best whiskey on the planet. Not state, not country, but planet. What started off as the mad scientist Chip Tate and his merry gang of innovators, Balcones has continued to turn out some unbelievable products since 2008.

Chip Tate is no longer at Balcones. When I swung by his new project and casually said that I was heading to Balcones after, he said, "well don't tell them you were here. I'm he who shall not be named." The break up wasn't the easiest, but I'm not going to get in to that... mostly because everyone told me far too much information and that saga is a book in and of itself. Break ups happen... who knows? Maybe we'll just end up with two world-class whiskey distilleries in Waco. That's what I'd like to think anyway.

Balcones 2.0 is doing just fine. They have always meticulously sought out ingredients for their richness in flavor. From blue corn grown in New Mexico to the first Texas-grown malted barley, every spirit they make aims for being recognizable and delectable. This translates to a delightful weight on the tongue, giving their whiskey a distinct density on the palate.

In 2011, they purchased the Texas Fireproof Storage Co. building in downtown Waco. Built in 1923, it is a massive structure of concrete, steel, and brick, and has 65,000 square feet of space (about 25 times larger than the first distillery). At the end of 2016, Balcones 2.0 officially opened their doors to the public and it's turned in to a great place to watch distilling happen. Balcones has made a significant investment not only in their operation, but also in their community of Waco.

I asked Jared Himstedt, Balcones head distiller, who freely admitted that he's not a cocktail guy, what cocktails he's seen with Balcones that have caught his eye. "There's always been some top-end mixologists that have done cool things with the Rumble... otherwise I love it when I see replacing tequila or mezcal with Brimstone. It's surprisingly cool." He took the words right out of my mouth. Balcones is available pretty much nationwide at your local enormous liquor store.

THE PEACEFUL PEOPLE

Balcones Distilling
Recipe: Maria Vieira from The East London Liquor Company in London, UK
225 S 11th St
Waco, TX 76701
(254) 755-6003
balconesdistilling.com

This one's fun. Balcones makes incredibly mixable spirits, and while they're brilliant alone, when given to a great bartender, they add complexities that can't be replicated.

Glassware: Clay Cups
Garnish: None

- 1.5 oz Balcones Baby Blue
- 1 teaspoon/barspoon mezcal
- .75 oz toasted butter pecan syrup
- .5 oz lemon juice
- 3 dashes of coffee bitters

1. Combine all ingredients and shake with ice.

2. Strain into traditional clay cups.

3. Serve with a side of blue corn bread with extra butter pecan syrup for dipping!

Toasted Butter Pecan Syrup

- **100 gr pecan halves**
- **300 gr/ml water**
- **260 g caster sugar**
- **10 ml melted butter**
- **2 g xantham gum, optional**

1. Moisturize the pecans in a solution of baking soda, water, and a pinch of sugar for 10 minutes.

2. Dry the pecans with a cloth and then toast them in the oven.

3. Crush the pecans and soak them in water to extract the oils and make a milk.

4. After 2 hours, blend the milk and pecans in a food processor.

5. Fine strain the liquid in a cheese cloth, gently squeezing by hand. You should have about 260 gr of toasted pecan milk at this point.

6. Add equal part of caster sugar (260 gr in this case) and mix it well until dissolved.

7. Add 10 ml of melted butter.

8. Add 2 gr of xantham gum.

THE BITTER POMELO

Cochineal
107 W San Antonio St
Marfa, TX 79843
(432) 729-3300
cochinealmarfa.com

Cochineal has been the go-to hot spot in Marfa for years. With Alexandra Gates taking over ownership in 2017, the tradition of frequent menu changes and seasonal offers carries on. Sabine said, "Alexandra and I are both European and grew up drinking Campari Orange or Aperol and have a love for bitter drinks and aperitifs. Because the restaurant also has a large garden where we grow lots of our own vegetables and all of our herbs, so we incorporate garden herbs in lots of drinks. So, we'd like to re-introduce our customers to the lost art of before-dinner drinks if you will, plus they stimulate and cleanse the palate."

Glassware: **Highball Glass**
Garnish: **Mint Sprig**

- **2 oz Cynar**
- **4 oz fresh Texas ruby red grapefruit juice**
- **3 to 5 mint leaves, crushed**

1. Mix all ingredients and stir until incorporated.

2. Strain into a highball and top off with Topo Chico.

3. Garnish with a sprig of mint.

HIBISCUS MARGARITA

Mexican Sugar
7501 Lone Star Dr B150
Plano, TX 75024
(972) 943-0984
mexicansugarcocina.com

I am, unashamedly, a draft cocktail nerd. If you've read this sucker cover to cover, you know why. The use of draft cocktails at Mexican Sugar is one of the coolest innovations in craft service that I've seen in a very long time. They have almost 20 draft cocktails on the menu! Coming from the folks behind Whiskey Cake and Ida Claire, Mexican Sugar is another entry into the suburban cocktail arena. The bar program is a tribute to all cocktails latin, utilizing ingredients like chica morada (Peruvian purple corn) or jicama juice or the inclusion of one of their massive collection of agave spirits. Also, this is a simple, tasty upgrade to your margarita.

Glassware: **Coupe Glass**
Garnish: **Lime Wheel**

- **1.75 oz reposado tequila**
- **.5 oz orange liqueur**
- **.75 oz hibiscus water**
- **.5 oz simple syrup**
- **.5 oz fresh lime juice**
- **Barspoon velvet falernum**

1. Combine ingredients in a shaker with ice and shake vigorously.

2. Fine strain into a chilled coupe glass.

3. Garnish with a lime wheel.

BOURBON COBBLER

Metropolitan
9181 Town Square Blvd Suite 1201
Amarillo, TX 79119
(806) 242-0117
metroofamarillo.com

Metropolitan is in Amarillo. You read that correctly. Amarillo. Cocktail culture has come to the panhandle, my friends. Playing off of historical speakeasies, there are some pretty humorous house rules that must be obeyed. "Don't bring anyone that you wouldn't bring to your mom's house on Sunday" is probably the one that we all should try to live by a little more often, but I digress. The color of this bourbon cobbler reminds me of an Amarillo sunset and is best consumed while watching one.

Glassware: **Wine Goblet**
Garnish: **Lemon Twist**

- **1.66 oz Eagle Rare bourbon**
- **.66 oz Luxardo Liquer**
- **.5 oz simple syrup**
- **3 peels each of lemon, orange, and grapefruit**

Stir all ingredients. Add a little ice and pour into a rocks-filled wine goblet.

—Dripping Springs—

"Are you from Texas originally?" Kevin Kelleher, founder of San Luis Spirits asked me.

"I am, sir, born and raised."

"Okay, then you'll get it then..."

San Luis Spirits, who makes Dripping Springs Vodka, was the second distiller in Texas.

Founded by brothers Gary and Kevin Kelleher, the company's first distribution was in April 2007. They're located in Dripping Springs, Texas, gateway to the Texas Hill Country.

"In 2006, it was a little more difficult than it would be (starting a distillery) today. It took 16 months, and until you have your license, you're not supposed to be doing anything, so you just did a bunch of planning and hoped it went through," Kevin told me.

"We started at a good time. We wound up sort of being the Pepsi to Tito's Coke. I will say that 10 years ago the acceptance of a Texas liquor brand didn't exist and didn't resonate with people. I wouldn't say it came naturally... but if you fast forward to today... because of Tito's, because of Deep Eddy, because of ourselves, because of Balcones, because of Garrison, because of some higher quality products, it turned into a way to a branding concept. It definitely is accepted as a place that makes great spirits, compared to what it used to be."

Then Kelleher's great aunt, who was originally from Russia (she was sent to Siberia by Catherine the Great for being German) used to tell them stories about how her grandfather was rumored to have made vodka for the Czar. Dripping Springs makes some of the most original vodka in Texas, made with artesian spring water and a Swedish activated charcoal filtration. It's balanced, with a smooth finish. They are distributed nationwide.

WATERMELON DAYS

Dripping Springs
5330 Bell Springs Rd
Dripping Springs, TX 78620
(512) 858-1199
drippingspringsvodka.com

This is a simple way to spice up a summer cocktail. You should make a big batch and head out to float the river.

Glassware: **Mason Jar**
Garnish: **Watermelon Slice**

- **2 oz Dripping Springs vodka**
- **Fresh watermelon pieces, chopped fine**
- **1 slice fresh jalapeño**
- **½ lime, juiced**

1. Place all ingredients into a shaker filled with ice.

2. Shake vigorously, pour into a mason jar, and garnish with a slice of watermelon.

OLD TIMER

Peggy's on the Green
128 W Blanco Rd
Boerne, TX 78006
(830) 572-5000
peggysonthegreen.com

Peggy's on the Green is named for the late mother of Chef/Owner Mark Bohanan, who was a great cook in her own right. Located in the historic Kendall Inn, an old stagecoach stop, Peggy's on the Green is from the founders of Bohanan's and the San Antonio Cocktail Conference. It's cocktails and elevated comfort food in the Hill County... I mean come on y'all... this is basically a Texan utopia.

Glassware: **Collins Glass**
Garnish: **Orange Zest**

- **1.5 oz bourbon**
- **.5 oz Cynar**
- **.5 oz Punt e Mes**
- **.5 oz lemon juice**
- **.25 oz simple syrup**
- **2-4 dashes Angostura bitters**
- **Top with soda**

Shake all ingredients. Double strain into collins glass filled with ice. Top with soda. Twist zest over drink and drop in.

—Tate & Company—

There aren't too many people in the world that have created such a following that they deserved to be talked about without an operable distillery. To peel back the curtain a bit... as I write this, it's "fall." The book, I've been told, comes out in "the spring." Tate & Company Distillery should be open by the time you read this. Or not. But regardless, if they're open, they're making some of the best products in the state. How do I know? It's Chip F-ing Tate.

In 2008, Chip Tate started Balcones. Balcones became one of the most reknowned, most awarded, most respected craft whiskey distilleries in the country, if not the world. They won 140 awards from 2010 to 2014. Also in August 2014, Tate and his investors found themselves in court. After the resulting legal battle, Chip was out and Balcones continued without his guidance.

Chip is now acknowledged as a leader in the craft distilling industry, having received more than 150 national and international awards, including US Craft Distillery of the Year and Global Distillery of the Year from the Wizards of Whisky International Competition. In recognition of his contributions to the development of the craft spirits industry, *Whisky Magazine* awarded him their inaugural Craft Whiskey Distillery of the Year Icon award in 2012, a category which he won again two years later. In 2013, The Spirits Business named him a Grand Master of World Whisky and in the following year, at the prestigious World Whisky Awards in London, he won the Best Overall American Whisky.

Chip's newest ventures, Tate & Company Distillery and Chip Tate Craft Copperworks, could very well end up being the most exciting chapter yet. Using the skills, expertise, and relationships he has developed to date, Chip is aspiring to make Tate & Company Distillery a haven for the craft movement, while his Tate Craft Copperworks is the world's first, distiller-led manufacturer and designer of artisanal copper pot stills. Together, Tate & Company Distillery and Chip Tate Craft Copperworks are creating and fostering a

new environment of creative collaboration for dedicated distillers around the world.

So here's what you have. Some cool pictures, and a promise of greatness... Whatever Tate & Company Distillery is selling, you should go buy.

—A CONVERSATION WITH—
Chip Tate

Alright man, let's start from the beginning…

Yes. Well, let's see, I really fell in love with cooking and fermentation when I was relatively young. Then in college I got into the brewing properly.

What was the first spirit that you made?

First spirits that I made were a honey and fig spirit and a blue corn whiskey. Some of that was strictly creative but some of that was philosophically intentional… With the whiskey, I wanted to make something that went out of its way to not be bourbon, but still something that was interesting to American whiskey drinkers. And the other was kind of the chef turned distiller…

We won't go into the why, but you're no longer at your original distillery. So, how about now? What are you up to now?

Well, we're building a quite remarkable craft distillery. It's going to be about the size of Balvenie, but with the capability to make just about anything. It'll allow us to do a lot of things that I've come up with but never had the capacity. For instance, I never felt like it would be okay to tinker with the stills when we're promising people bottles they couldn't get of stuff we already sold them.

I'm sure they appreciated that. Are you incorporating anything particularly exciting?

We've got some cool cooperative projects that I can't go into yet that cross state and national borders. We're really trying to just set up a good, strong, long-term craft distillery that we'll be able to look back 20 years from now and say this is a stable thing.

What's been your biggest challenge with the new distillery?

This is hard and expensive and time-consuming and expensive to set up a distillery to actually produce some things measured in millions. We have two 2,500 gallons in a direct fire pot stills with interesting mixing manifolds and infrared burners. We have four double steam jacketed spirit stills. We have a full malt kit small we're about to break ground on a 50,000 square foot rickhouse that I already know is going to be too small.

Did you ever consider leaving Texas?

Hell no, absolutely not. My house is here, all my friends are here, why would I leave? Besides, I need to make sure there's at least one good distillery here.

Miller

Ironroot Republic Distillery

According to *Whisky Magazine,* which may have some pedigree in these sorts of things, the world's best corn whiskey comes from Ironroot Republic Distillery in Denison. "We love our whiskey," Robert Likarish, co-founder of Ironroot, said. "We think it's great, but for a distillery our age to be as young as we are to win an award like this is completely unheard of."

Ironroot is Texas, through and through... run by Texans, making Texas spirits, using Texas grain. From grain to glass, as they say, Ironroot is one of the most impressive operations in the state. They're creative in all the right ways. Creative use of grains? Yep. Obsession with locality of source materials? Oh yeah. Funky barrel-aging techniques? I had one they finished in both port and Islay barrels... so yes. Good lord, yes.

One of the weirder and cooler things that I learned about at Ironroot was starka. Starka is barrel-aged vodka and has been popular in Eastern Europe since the 15th century. Families would bury barrels of starka when a child was born and then when it was their wedding day, they'd dig it up and party. Ironroot is making Texas starka and it's pretty interesting... It's similar to a whiskey and the spirit certainly pulls flavors out of the wood — vanilla, caramel, chocolate, and fruit, but it's definitely an aged vodka. Give it a try.

This is a family affair. Along with Robert, his brother Jonathan is the co-founder and head distiller, and their mom keeps the boys in line. The biggest outlier here, to me, is the training... these guys initially trained in cognac and then wound up spending a lot of time with Chip Tate down in Waco. They're taking techniques that aren't traditionally used for whiskey and making some of the best corn whiskey on the planet with it. Jonathan said, "How we run the stills is a lot closer to the way that the French run their cognac stills than American whiskey."

This is an exceptional distillery. Their creativity seemingly has no bounds. Of all of the whiskey joints in Texas, this is one to watch.

Ironroot Republic Distillery
3111 Loy Lake Rd
Denison, TX 75020
(903) 337-0495

ironrootrepublic.com

THE WOODSTOCK MULE

CHASE'S PLACE COCKTAILS + KITCHEN
313 E. San Antonio St.
Fredericksburg, TX 78624
(830) 320-9020
chasesplacecocktails.com

When you come to visit the beautiful Texas whiskey and wine region, an absolute must visit is Chase's Place. With some of the best food and absolutely the best cocktails in the Hill Country, Chase and Tara Guthrie have created the perfect way to end your day of wine and whiskey tasting. The Woodstock Mule features Highway Texas Vodka (Texas' first Black-owned distillery out of Houston) and is a fun way to experiment with CBD in your cocktails.

Glassware: **Rocks Glass**

Garnish: **Chaste Tree Leaf (or Hemp Leaf), Lime Wedge**

- **2 oz CBD Flower and Fresh Ginger-Infused Highway Hemp-Seed Vodka**
- **.75 oz fresh lime juice**
- **Greenbelt Pineapple Turmeric Kombucha, to top**

1. Combine vodka and lime in a shaker with ice, shake vigorously, and pout into the glass.

2. Top with kombucha and garnish with leaf and lime wedge.

CBD Flower and Fresh Ginger Infused Vodka

- .25 oz Indica CBD Flower
- Fresh ginger, to taste
- 1 bottles Highway Texas Hemp Vodka

1. Combine all ingredients in a container with a lid and let stand for at least 24 hours, 72 hours for optimal terpene profile extraction.
2. Strain and store.

Turbinado Syrup

- 2 parts turbinado sugar
- 1 part hot water

Combine and stir until sugar is completely dissolved.

PORTER FLIP

Preamble Lounge & Craft House
Recipe: Sage Sharp
20801 Gulf Fwy #12
Webster, TX 77598
(832) 905-2927
preamblelounge.com

As of late, beer cocktails have become a great addition to today's on cocktail programs. It's a collection of flavor profiles that you can play with if your bar also has a great beer selection, like so many quality programs today do. At Preamble in Webster, they make a remarkable flip with a coffee porter base. 8th Wonder is a great Houston brewery and if you can get it, their Rocket Fuel porter is perfect in this cocktail. Suburban cocktails man, I'm telling you... these places are the future.

Glassware: **Coupe Glass**
Garnish: **Ground Cinnamon**

- **2 oz 8th Wonder Rocket Fuel Vietnamese coffee porter (flattened)**
- **1.5 oz spiced rum**
- **1 oz turbinado syrup**
- **1 whole egg**

1. Combine all ingredients and dry shake without ice for 10 seconds.

2. Shake with ice for 30 seconds.

3. Fine mesh strain into a coupe glass.

4. Garnish with ground cinnamon.

—Garrison Brothers Distillery—

Garrison Brothers made some of the first whiskey in Texas. In fact, they were the 29th distillery in the United States (now there are over 1500) and they were literally having to explain to regulatory entities how distilling works and what they should be looking for when they come to do an inspection. Dan Garrison, the founder, had approached Tito Beveridge multiple times about starting a distillery. "I know he wanted to make whiskey and I told him I was going to, but [I] think he didn't believe me," laughed Garrison.

In 2004, Dan Garrison walked away from a financially rewarding but volatile career as a software marketing professional. After numerous trips to Kentucky to learn how to make bourbon, Garrison set up shop on his small farm and ranch in the Hill Country. He borrowed money from friends and family. He built a small "experimental barn" and began tinkering with equipment, tanks, pumps, plumbing, steam, barrels, grain, and yeast. In November 2007, he bought an antique pot still named The Copper Cowgirl who was originally built in 1972 for Wild Turkey.

The following year, Garrison uncorked one of the bourbon barrels, tasted the 7 month old bourbon, and immediately began to beg, borrow, and steal to build a bigger distillery. Since then, bottles of Garrison Brothers Texas Straight Bourbon Whiskey has become quite sought after. Five vintages have been released and each has sold out in a matter of days, and when a new release is announced, bourbon drinkers road-trip to the Hill Country to get one.

Garrison is proud of his bourbon. It's expensive and Garrison is quick to defend that. The entire time we were chatting it felt like he was alluding to something. "Honor the spirit." "Why would anyone want to put something in bourbon?" "Cocktails are alright but I drink bourbon." "Once you add something, it's not bourbon." So I asked him…

"Dan. Do you hate cocktails?"

He said, "No, absolutely not. I tend to be a little bit of an antago-

nist, but I am the first person to admit that I know next to nothing about making a great cocktail. Zero. Zilch. Nada. My standard go-to is a Garrison Brothers on the rocks with a splash of Topo Chico, served in a 32-ounce YETI Rambler. I can sip on one of those for days."

Unfortunately for Dan, Garrison Brothers Texas Straight Bourbon Whiskey makes some damn fine drinks. So we'll include two of them... the one that Dan recommends and the one that we do.

The Perfect Garrison

- Two parts Garrison Brothers Texas Straight Bourbon Whiskey
- One part glass

REV'S HILL COUNTRY DONKEY

Garrison Brothers Distilling
Recipe: Jason P. Brand, Garrison Brothers Distillery, Hye, Texas
1827 Hye-Albert Rd
Hye, TX 78635
(830) 392-0246
garrisonbros.com

"After working an event in Austin one hot-as-hell summer day, I was on my way back to the still house in Hye. Needing a break on this grueling hour-and-a-half drive, I decided to stop by a "hole in the wall" bar for a drink. As I sat down at the bar I noticed a young hipster couple drinking something out of cold, sweaty copper mugs. Now, as a distiller I have a fondness for copper, because copper is shiny, and Rev loves shiny things. I asked what it was, and the bartender told me it was a Moscow Mule, which is made with vodka. Well, frankly, vodka sucks. I once heard a wise man say 'vodka is intended for rich women on diets.' I have to agree. Still, wanting to get a drink from the cold, shiny copper mug and noticing they had our bourbon behind the bar, I asked if he would mind replacing the dietary supplement with Garrison Brothers Texas Straight Bourbon, and add extra lime juice. Rev's Hill Country Donkey was born!"—Reverend Jason Brand, Distillery Director, Garrison Brothers.

Glassware: **Copper Mug**
Garnish: **Lime Wedge**

- **2.5 oz Garrison Brothers Texas Straight bourbon whiskey**
- **Juice from half of lime**
- **Fever Tree or your favorite ginger beer**

1. Fill copper mug with crushed ice.
2. Add ginger beer, bourbon, and lime juice.
3. Lime wedge on rim as garnish.
4. For an extra kick, use spicy ginger beer!

ROCA PATRÓN.

PITAYA-RITA

Salt New American Table
Recipe: Daniel Copado
210 N Main St
McAllen, TX 78504
(956) 627-6304
saltnewamericantable.com

Location, location, location. Your cocktails, like your food, should be different, contingent on where you are consuming them. It's a key element in the way Chef Larry Delgado runs Salt in McAllen, but it has brilliantly impacted the bar program as well. The Pitaya-rita is a valley cocktail through and through. It begins with Pitaya Farms dragon fruit from Raymondville, Texas, and Texas Valley lemons from Hernandez Farms in Weslaco, Texas, This is about as local as you can get... but if Pitaya dragon fruit isn't available, whatever you can find will do just fine.

Glassware: **Rocks Glass**
Garnish: **Dragon Fruit Slice**

- **1.5 oz Chefs Select Patron reposado**
- **1 oz dragon fruit puree**
- **1.25 oz Texas Valley lemons**
- **.75 oz agave nectar**
- **.75 oz Gran Marnier**

1. Combine ingredients in a shaker with ice and shake vigorously.

2. Strain into a rocks glass.

3. Garnish with a slice of dragon fruit.

—Tabernilla—

7124 Bob Bullock Loop
Laredo, TX 78041
(956) 723-7400
TABERNILLALAREDO.COM

Bartenders are my people. I love it when someone with the right kind of talent decides to make cocktails/spirits/bartending their career. That being said, there's something kinda cool about a chef who'll step behind a bar and come up with something. Tabernilla Tapas Bar is a lively tapas restaurant run by Chef Robert Gonzales, a local from Laredo who took off to work in massive programs in New York and Dallas. The cocktail program is, naturally, Spanish heavy with multiple sangrias and a good array of espresso-driven cocktails. It's creative and fun, but not too out there.

LA BUENA VERBENA

Don't be afraid when you see multiple ingredients, they are all useful outside of these recipes. The sweet lemon verbena tea you're about to make is delicious. Make extra.

Glassware: **Coupe**
Garnish: **Lemon Verbena Leaf**

- **1.25 oz Hendrick's gin**
- **.5 oz key lime juice**
- **1 oz lemon verbena tea**
- **.25 oz saffron syrup**

1. Chill a mixing glass with ice or in refrigerator prior to use.

2. Add ingredients to mixing glass and stir until very cold.

3. Pour liquid into a chilled thin coupe glass.

4. Grab a large lemon verbena leaf and make a small slice down the center large enough to allow you to place the leaf on the rim.

Saffron Syrup

- **⅛ tsp crushed Spanish saffron stems**
- **1 cup water**
- **1 cup natural cane sugar**

Bring water, sugar, and saffron to a boil and immediately turn off heat. Let syrup stand until completely cool, then store in refrigerator.

Sweet Lemon Verbena Tea

- **8 oz water**
- **2 oz natural cane sugar**
- **6 large lemon verbena leaves**

Bring water and sugar to boil then add lemon verbena leaves. Let steep 20 minutes then strain and let completely cool. Store refrigerated.

— Hye Rum —

I'm a sucker for good wine. I always have been. One of my favorite wineries in Texas was this little hole-in-the-wall place in Deep Ellum (Dallas) called Calais. Ben Calais is a Frenchman turned Texan who can blend the hell out of some wine. Try the Syrah, the Bordeaux, and the Cab Franc to have your mind blown. In fact, this is the Texas wine I usually use in the "Alright pal, I've got some Texas wine, let's do a blind taste test" type challenges that will occasionally appear.

But enough about wine… a few years ago, Ben told me that he was moving to Hye, keeping up his winery, but also going to start making rum. Enter Hye Rum. I got a chance to chat with his co-founder and head distiller, James Davidson, about all things Hye and rum.

So why did you get in to distilling?

About 8 years ago, my Father said he wanted to open a whiskey distillery. I started to study Scotch and other whiskies. I would go to every branding event in the area and joined Scotch groups in order to learn more. While I was widening my pallet, I learned to distill via the internet and books.

How did you and Ben meet?

Ben and I met in 2011 at a pot-luck style dinner party a mutual friend organized. Ben wanted to make rum, but was too busy with his winery to learn to distill and start another business. At the time, I had no experience (or interest) in rum. I just figured it was a random conversation with a guy about the beverage business.

No interest in rum huh? So why the change of heart?

After that conversation, I decided to taste rum. The established "good" rums that a lot of people seemed to like were okay, but seemed overly sweet. After that, I tried some craft rums and they lacked the robust flavor I was used to from drinking Scotch.

Next time I saw Ben, I reported my experience to him. Ben gave me the names of some rums from the French Islands and Jamaica. When I finally secured a couple bottles, I was impressed. They had a lot of flavor and varied greatly from everything else I had tried.

It puzzled me that craft distillers were making near vodka-like rums when the medium had so much to offer. This was a huge motivator for me to move from whiskey to rum. My father often said to me in my youth, "If you don't like it, make it yourself." I felt I could do better then what was readily available.

So why Hye?

It wasn't until 2013 that Ben and I made a hard commitment to pursue a joint venture together. Ben had already purchased land in Hye, Texas for his winery and was in the process of moving there. The wine trail had a lot of traffic and we figured we could catch some of it. Also, Hye was becoming known for some good wineries and Garrison Brother's. We looked in Hye and the surrounding area for 2–3 years before we found our location.

PIÑA COLADA

Hye Rum
11247 U.S. 290
Hye, TX 78671
(830) 265-5644
hyerum.com

Nothing beats a good piña colada.This is a particularly cool way to serve this classic, and the rum blend is perfect.

Glassware: **Hurricane Glass**
Garnish: **orange slice and a tiny umbrella**

- **3 oz creme of coconut**
- **3 oz pineapple juice**
- **1 oz of Hye White Rum**
- **1.5 oz Hye Dark Rum float on top**

1. Blend all ingredients for 30 plus seconds with ice.

2. Serve in a hurricane glass and garnish with an orange slice and a tiny umbrella.

—ANC Alchemy—

Ashley Compton is an East Coast girl turned... Marfaite? Marfinian? She lives in Marfa. Since 2009, Ashley has been making herb-based tinctures, bitters, and various honeys. In 2012, she moved to Marfa and the diversity of her options for ingredients changed dramatically. It opened up a whole new arena of medicinal plants and botanical fauna and has changed the way she's gone about utilizing the natural elements in her work.

All of her products are made in small batches and contain desert-foraged herbs. She also uses chihuahuan desert honey and organic medicinals to flush out the palette of flavors. The bitters are quite unique, which is sometimes hard to do in a bitter, and they provide incredible complexity to cocktails or coffee drinks.

Funny side note, in my past life I was the program director of an indie rock station in Dallas and I got to know Ashley's husband, Andy, when his band Wye Oak played in studio for us. "Civilian" is still one of the greatest songs ever written. But I digress... Ashley was nice enough to provide a recipe for her Brushfire bitters... ANC Alchemy bitters are available online through her website.

WEST TEXAS BRUSHFIRE BITTERS

ANC Alchemy
anc-alchemy.com

Ashley was nice enough to provide a full recipe from gathered ingredients to use in cocktails. This bitters is incredible in an Old Fashioned, particularly when using an agave spirit.

- **2 cups overproof bourbon**
- **1 cup dried elderflower**
- **½ arbol chile, dried**
- **½ ancho chile, dried**
- **1/16 cup epazote**
- **⅛ cup rosemary, dried**
- **20 juniper berries**
- **¼ cup bitter orange, dried peel**
- **¼ tsp gentian**
- **⅛ tsp black walnut leaf**
- **2 teaspoons honey**

1. In a quart-sized glass jar, combine all of the dried ingredients. Cover with the bourbon and shake well. Let stand in a darkened, cool space for 2 weeks. Shake daily.

2. Strain the infused bourbon into another clean, 1-quart glass jar through cheesecloth. Squeeze any infused alcohol from the cheesecloth into the jar—reserving the solids. Strain again the infused bourbon through new cheesecloth into another clean jar to remove any remaining sediment. Cover the jar and set aside for 1 week.

3. Meanwhile, transfer the solids to a small saucepan. Add 1 cup of water, bring to a boil. Cover and simmer over low heat for 10 minutes; let cool. Pour the combined liquid and solids into a clean, 1-quart glass jar. Cover and let stand in a cool, dark space for 1 week. Shake daily.

4. Double-strain the water mixture through a cheesecloth-lined funnel set over a clean 1-quart glass jar; discard the solid herbs material. Add the infused alcohol and the syrup. Cover and let stand at room temperature for 3 days. Pour the bitters through cheesecloth or strainer. Funnel into 2 or 4 oz dropper bottles. Use to enhance and alchemically-coagulate drinks, or to create a bittered digestif when added to club soda.

DESERT SPOON

The Blue Door
Recipe: Erica Mann
4610 N Garfield St D
Midland, TX 79705
(432) 218-8793

Sotol means Desert Spoon. Now that we have that covered, I'm so glad there are a few sotol cocktails in this book. Maybe by the end of it, I'll have you convinced that you should give it a try. The Blue Door is at its core a neighborhood bar. In the five years they have been open, they have developed a family that gives back to the community, cheers each other's marriages, babies, and promotions, and supports each other through sickness, hard knocks, and loss. It's kinda like it's a great neighborhood bar in a small(er) Texas town. Owner Erica Mann said, "Being able to experience all of this while also introducing our region to fizzes, egg whites, and crustas, is the cherry in my Manhattan."

Glassware: **Coupe Glass**
Garnish: **Rosemary Sprig**

- **2 oz sotol reposado**
- **.5 oz Cointreau**
- **2 oz ruby red grapefruit juice**
- **1 oz lime juice**
- **.5 oz agave syrup**

1. Combine ingredients in a shaker with ice and shake vigorously.

2. Strain into a coupe glass.

3. Garnish with a fresh rosemary sprig.

—A CONVERSATION WITH—
Jason Kosmas

Why would someone who owns one of the hottest bars in New York City move to Dallas?

It was my wife, Carolyn's, mother actually. She had just gone through a divorce and moved back to Texas. Carolyn decided to be with her mom during that time. That was right around the time I realized I was in love with her. She was going back and forth for a couple months and finally says, "Hey, guess what? I moved to Texas."

Long story short, I convinced her to move back to New York, and we opened Employees Only. Then we opened up Macao Trading Company, and then Lola, my first daughter, was born and that was when things really started to change.

So, you moved to Dallas?

I had a plan to do an Employees Only in Austin, back in 2007 or 2008. But It didn't seem like it was a good time for Austin. The culinary movement hadn't really started yet. It wasn't really out there. When I talk to bartenders, they usually have two jobs at least, to make ends meet. Dallas made more sense. We were working on The 86 Co. [Kosmas' spirits company that makes delicious rum, vodka, gin, and tequila] already, and I was writing our cocktail book, *Speakeasy,* pretty ferociously at that time.

How long were you in Dallas and what brought the move to Austin?

My daughter was getting close to a kindergarten. We were like, "Okay, we need to figure out schools..." And all of sudden, Carolyn and I both said, "I think I'm ready to move on." We were still talking about moving to Austin, but in about two years... but then we have that moment. We're like, "Okay. Once she goes in the school, we're not going to move in a few years." If we want to do this--

Austin is incredible. I really love it. The kids love their school, because it was perfect. I got to know most of the people in bars and restaurants here. Austin is great.

To you, what is a Texas cocktail?

That's a pretty good question. I think Texas cocktails are approachable--they're fun and people go out to drink and have a good time. And what's cool to see is the bartenders here getting to sneak a little creativity and ingenuity into them. In general, I think people in Texas are converting more people into cocktail lovers than either of the coasts.

I mean, look at the restaurants scene. It feels like every restaurant in Texas has a cocktail menu.

And you look at people in Dallas and in Houston, they dine out four nights a week, easily. They're being exposed to it on such a daily basis, more so than people who only go to very pristine cocktail bars. This is the masses. Texas is the democratizing the cocktail.

The whole process of The 86 Company was to grow a cocktail culture and we wanted to help the places who are making cocktails specifically. Then when I moved to Dallas it changed my world and my perspective. I started thinking, "We need to show everybody that cocktails are easy to make." Everyone at the end of the day deserves a good cocktail.

TEQUILA BLACKBERRY SMASH

Locality
Recipe: Matthew Barrington
1010 Halsell St
Bridgeport, TX 76426
(214) 686-6500
facebook.com/localitybridgeport

Locality is in the sleepy town of Bridgeport. This is another example of how you don't have to be in a major market to have a truly elevated cocktail experience. Locality has made plenty of waves since opening and has hosted a series of pop-up charity events to further solidify their place in Wise County. Incredible cocktails in a small Texas town sounds like heaven if you ask me. The blackberry smash is a riff on the classic cocktail, the bramble, and is heavily reliant on fresh blackberries. This cocktail is also the reason no one can get blackberries in Bridgeport, because Matthew is constantly buying everything they have. Don't blame me! I just work here...

Glassware: **Cantarito or Clay Mug**
Garnish: **Lime Wheel, Blackberry**

- **5-6 blackberries**
- **1.5 oz simple syrup**
- **2 oz blanco tequila**
- **1.5 oz fresh lime juice**
- **.5 oz St. George Raspberry Liqueur**
- **4-5 dashes Fee Bros Plum Bitters**

1. Muddle blackberries in a cocktail shaker with simple syrup. Add remaining ingredients, shake vigorously with ice, and strain into mug.

2. Top with crushed ice and garnish with a lime wheel and blackberry.

OLD PAL MARGARITA

Old Pal Bar
100 E Market St
Lockhart, TX 78644
instagram.com/oldpaltx/

Old Pal is one of those bars that you see in movies, but you're fairly confident don't actually exist. A tequila- and whiskey-focused cocktail bar and honky-tonk in Lockhart, the BBQ capital of the world? Come on man—that wouldn't even fly on Ted Lasso. But it's very real and it's incredibly well done. Travis Tober, of Nickel City fame, teamed up with Rich Reimbolt of Better Half, also in Austin, to conjure up one of the most Texas-y bars we've got. If you find yourself in Lockhart on a BBQ adventure, this is an absolute must visit. Not fancy, but always stellar, we give you the Old Pal Margarita. The twist is a squeeze of key lime, which affects the ph balance and makes the margarita damn near chuggable! This is best paired with fried chicken or the beef rib from Black's down the street.

Glassware: **Rocks Glass**
Garnish: **Lime Wedge**

- **2oz Altos Blanco Tequila**
- **Juice of 1 Mexican lime**
- **Juice of 1 key lime**
- **.5 oz organic agave**

1. Combine all ingredients in a cocktail shaker with ice, shake vigorously, and strain into the glass.

2. Garnish with lime wedge.

BEST OF *Texas*

I've always been a fan of those alt-weekly newspaper's "best of" sections they'll do at the end of every year. "Best ham sandwich on a patio that serves Frosè" or "Best resale shop specializing in toddler-sized band shirts." You know the drill. So here's the best of section for the great state of Texas. Just know, the best of the best in Texas is like the best of the best in anything else... it's your preference and taste that matter the most. If you think it's the best, then by golly, it's the best.

BEST
POOLSIDE COCKTAIL EXPERIENCE

Hibiscus Syrup

- 600 ml sugar
- 350 ml water
- 200 ml hibiscus

1. Combine all ingredients in a saucepan over medium-high heat and bring to a boil, stirring until the sugar dissolves. Cook until the color is a deep burgundy and the liquid can coat the back of a spoon.

2. Strain and store. It will keep in the refrigerator for 2 weeks, but add half a shot of vodka to make it last for up to a month.

EL PAJARO

Space Cowboy
100 W Cavalcade St
Houston, TX 77009
spacecowboyhou.com

Space Cowboy is a fun and quirky poolside oasis with tropical drinks and amazing Filipino-style food. Samantha Ruiz's riff on the classic 70s tropical cocktail the "Jungle Bird" is named after a card in the Mexican bingo game, Loteria. The bittersweet and tart hibiscus syrup is balanced out by the sweetness of the fresh pineapple juice.

Glassware: **Collins Glass**

Garnish: **Bruleed Pineapple, Mint Sprigs, El Pajaro Loteria Card**

- **Orange juice, to top**
- **.25 oz fresh lime juice**
- **1 oz fresh pineapple juice**
- **.5 oz Hibiscus Syrup**
- **.25 oz Apaluz Mezcal**
- **.75 oz Campari**
- **1 oz white rum**

1. Use blender to "fluff" the orange juice and set aside.

2. Build the cocktail in the Collins glass and top with crushed ice, leaving a ½ inch space.

3. Slowly pour the fluffy orange juice over the crushed ice and garnish with a bruleed pineapple (add sugar to a pineapple wedge and torch), mint sprigs, and a El Pajaro card attached to the glass with a colorful clothespin.

AMY JO JOHNSON

This is the Amy Jo Johnson and in case you didn't grow up in the mid-1990s, that's the name of the Pink Power Ranger. The drink is a bit spicy and smokey because of the mezcal, a bit sweet and sour because of the shrub, and, appropriately, pink. But it'll kick your butt if you're not careful.

Glassware: **Rocks Glass**
Garnish: **Strawberry and Basil**

- **1.5 oz mezcal**
- **1 strawberry**
- **3 basil leaves**
- **.75 oz lime juice**
- **.75 oz simple syrup**
- **1 tsp ume shrub (2 parts umeshu plum wine and 1 part balsamic)**

1. Muddle strawberry and basil.

2. Add ingredients and ice to shaker and shake vigorously.

3. Strain into a rocks glass.

4. Garnish with strawberry and basil.

BEST
COCKTAILS AT
A RAMEN
PLACE

—Ninja Ramen—

4219 WASHINGTON AVE
HOUSTON, TX 77007
(281) 888-5873
NINJARAMEN.COM

Ramen and cocktails. A combination that should from hence forth shall never be separated again. Well, if Christopher Huang could have his way, it wouldn't be. Ninja Ramen is super local, incredibly creative. Chris told me that on a trip to Taiwan he went to a series of bars and saw these magical concoctions in coupes everywhere. "I thought, that's it! I'll come back to Houston and I'll open a cocktail bar! We don't have one of those. But by the time I got back and I got invited to this place called Anvil… I decided to regroup and work ramen in to the plan," he told me chuckling.

BEST
DRAFT COCKTAILS IN A FOOD TRUCK PARK

—Truckyard—

5624 SEARS ST
DALLAS, TX 75206
(469) 500-0139
TRUCKYARDDALLAS.COM

When Truckyard hit the Dallas scene, the reaction was overwhelming. Imagine that? Texans loved the idea of craft beer, quick craft cocktails (Truckyard uses a lot of batched cocktails, either utilizing draft systems or often bottling cocktails), and a huge yard full of nothing but park benches and food trucks, all under massive shade trees. It's a patio to end all patios. It's a Texas-style beer garden with decent cocktails. It's one of the easiest places to be. Why didn't we have this since… ever? This isn't rocket science, people, come on. Now, thankfully, Truckyard has reminded everyone just how important a Texas patio is. Inside, they have… 10 seats? I think? Maybe 20, tops. Outside, it's Texas. Beer drinking, Paloma sipping, two-stepping (when there's a band on), Texas.

FROZEN COCONUT KEY LIME PIE

We give you the Frozen Coconut Key Lime Pie, the easiest way to impress your friends. And because you should never make just one frozen drink, this is party sized for 8 folks. Or 4 folks. Or just you. I ain't judging. Serves 8.

Glassware: **Pint Glass**
Garnish: **Lime Wedge**

- **1½ cups (12 oz) Keke key lime pie liqueur**
- **½ cup (4 oz) Rumhaven coconut water rum**
- **6 tbsp (3 oz) lime juice**
- **2 tbsp sugar**
- **4 cups (32 oz) coconut water**

1. Add all ingredients to blender with 2 cups ice.
2. Blend and serve.

— Liber & Co —

Robert and Adam Higginbotham started to see the writing on the wall around 2011. Robert told me, "we noticed that something was missing. While high-end spirits, liqueurs, and bitters meant that everyone could obtain most of what's needed to make better cocktails, there was still a problem for the discerning drinker. An entire ingredient category remained overlooked."

Liber & Co is an absolute requirement for the home bartender. Their gum syrups, grenadine, and orgeat can hang among any housemade versions you'll find. If you need a syrup and Liber & Co. makes it, you're good. These are some of the best cocktail syrups in the country, let alone the state. Liber & Co. is available statewide, as well as a few other states, but are rapidly expanding.

No one offered a way to translate the craft cocktails that people were starting to have out in the wild, so they jumped in. It started as a personal project with all of the founders in three different places, and once they had that first order, they knew they had something. "HEB. That's when I knew it was real. We got our first order from HEB," said Robert, "They're amazing. They try to work specifically with local companies and they support the little guy."

If you see a picture of these guys, you may recognize them from

Billion Dollar Buyer on CNBC. Producers of the reality show reached out to Liber & Co. with the opportunity to pitch Tillman Fertitta, the owner of Landry's, who operates over 500 properties in 36 states and had just bought this little basketball team in Houston… the Rockets.

"It goes from very low expectations to finding out we were selected… it was crazy. We didn't know anything about TV. We barely knew about the show and now we're wrestling with our landlord to get permission for them to be around for a month," said Robert. "It was weird. It was fun, but it was weird."

GIN BASIL SMASH

Liber & Co
2204 Forbes Dr Suite 103
Austin, TX 78754
liberandcompany.com

Fresh basil shines in this simple cocktail and perfectly complements gin's botanicals. This quick and easy cocktail is an example of how using quality ingredients will make you look like you've got the goods!

Glassware: **Rocks Glass**
Garnish: **Fresh Basil**

- **.5 oz Classic Gum Syrup**
- **2 oz gin**
- **2–3 sprigs fresh basil**
- **.75 oz lemon juice**

1. Muddle basil and syrup in a shaker tin.

2. Add lemon juice, gin, and ice and shake for 10 seconds.

3. Fine strain into an ice filled rocks glass.

4. Garnish with a basil leaf.

BEST
WAY TO LOOK LIKE
A MIXOLOGY PRO,
EVEN IF YOU
DON'T KNOW
ANYTHING

BEST BAR
IN AN ALLEY

THE RUM DIARY

Atwater Alley
4900 McKinney Ave
Dallas, TX 75205
(469) 893-9400
atwateralley.com

While the "speakeasy" trend is waning, thankfully, one of the best bars in Dallas is still one you'll have to find. In fact, go to their website and all you'll see is a logo and the words "find me." The entrance to Atwater Alley is inside of one. You legitimately have to walk down an alley to an unmarked door. The doorman tends to give the secret away, but it's still pretty cool, nonetheless. Once inside, it's a two-story, cocktail-driven den that absolutely gives you the feeling that only the cool kids know about this one. Their cocktail, The Rum Diary, is slightly bitter but so smooth you'll be making another before you're done with your first.

Glassware: **Coupe Glass**
Garnish: **Lemon Peel**

- **2 oz Brugal 1888**
- **.5 oz Amaro Nonino**
- **.5 oz Aperol**
- **2 dashes Agnostura bitters**

1. Combine all ingredients in a mixing glass.

2. Add ice and stir for 15–30 seconds with a bar spoon.

3. Strain into a coupe and garnish with a lemon peel.

THREE EMMAS COCKTAIL

Sternewirth at Hotel Emma
136 E Grayson St
San Antonio, TX 78215
(210) 223-7375
thehotelemma.com/culinary/sternewirth

Hotel Emma is, and I say this with no hesitation, the most beautiful hotel I've ever stepped foot into. And hospitality is imperative at their incredible bar, Sternewirth. A dramatic 25-foot vaulted ceiling soars over intimate groupings of sofas, easy chairs, and banquettes arranged to encourage conversation and celebration. Their name-sake cocktail is a tribute to the old Pearl Brewery, in which the hotel now resides. This is the crown jewel of the Pearl district in San Antonio, which may be the crown jewel district in town. Hotel Emma needs to be a bucket list vacation spot. It's truly special.

Glassware: **Nick & Nora**
Garnish: **Basil Leaf**

- **1 oz Pearl Beer and Rose cordial**
- **1 oz Amontillado sherry**
- **.75 oz Botanist gin**
- **.5 oz lemon juice**
- **.5 oz grapefruit juice**

1. Shake all ingredients together, and strain into glass over fresh cracked ice.

2. Garnish with a basil leaf.

Pearl and Rose Cordial

- **8 12-oz Pearl beers**
- **12 cups sugar**

1. Slowly pour beer in pot to avoid becoming too foamy. Add the sugar into the pot and turn on low until sugar dissolves. Do not let it get to a full boil.

2. Turn off heat and let cool.

3. Add 36.5 oz rose cordial.

4. Add 2.5 oz rose water.

5. Put into deli containers, label, and date.

Rock Candy Syrup

- .5 cup water
- 1 cup turbinado sugar
- 1 cinnamon stick
- 2 cloves

1. Bring water to a boil in a saucepan over medium heat, add sugar and stir until it dissolves.

2. Add the cinnamon stick and cloves, bring back up to a boil, and reduce heat. Simmer for 15 minutes.

3. Remove from heat to allow to cool before pouring into a bottle or container. Refrigerate for up to a month.

MARTIKI 2.0

Swizzle
1802 Greenville Ave #110
Dallas, TX 75206
(469) 862-3102
swizzledallas.com

There's been a delightful increase in the amount of quality tropical and tiki bars across the state as of late. Swizzle opened in the midst of the pandemic and while the grand plans were slightly dampened, Swizzle has become an oasis in the midst of the craziness of Lower Greenville in Dallas. What started out as a five-year pop-up became a passion project for couple and owners Jen and Marty Reyes. This Beachcomber bar that will transport you to a tropical place and the Martiki 2.0 will finish the job. Nothing like a good tiki drink!

Glassware: **Tiki Mug or Collins Glass**
Garnish: **Swizzle Stick, Three Pineapple Leaves, Bendy Straw**

- **1 oz unaged overproof Jamaican rum**
- **.5 oz Rock Candy Syrup**
- **.5 oz fresh lime juice**
- **1.5 oz pineapple juice**
- **.5 oz demerara rum, to float**

1. Combine all ingredients, except demerara rum, in glass, add pebble or crushed ice, and swizzle until frost forms on outside of the glass. Top off with more ice.

2. Garnish with a swizzle stick, pineapple leaves, and straw, and then add rum float.

LOST CAUSE

Alexandre's
4026 Cedar Springs Rd
Dallas, TX 75219
(214) 559-0720
alexandres.com

Located in the center of Dallas's LGBT community, Alexandre's is shotgun-style live music venue. While bars along Cedar Springs Road serve as a refuge for the community, for the past 17 years Alexandre's also gives refuge to cocktail enthusiasts away from the dance clubs that dominate the street. Industry veteran Jordan Robinson created the Lost Cause on the fly for a customer wanting something new. Robinson passed away in 2019, but his legacy is his many cocktails still being served today, like this one that is little bitter, a little sweet, with enough alcohol to get the point across.

Glassware: **Rocks Glass**
Garnish: **Flamed Orange Zest**

- **2 muddled strawberries**
- **1.5 oz Aperol**
- **0.75 oz Flor de Cana 4yr Extra Dry**
- **0.75 oz Cointreau**
- **1 oz simple syrup**
- **1 oz fresh lemon juice**

1. Muddle the strawberries in a cocktail shaker.

2. Combine remaining ingredients in the shaker with ice, shake vigorously, and strain into a rocks glass.

3. Garnish with flamed orange zest.

BEST
PLACE TO CELEBRATE
LGBTQ PRIDE

BEST
Way to Escape Dirty Sixth and Have a World-Class Cocktail

Dijon Syrup (aka Buck Sauce)

- 4 cups honey
- 3 tsps sweet smoked paprika
- 16 tbsp (heaping) Dijon mustard
- 4 oz hot water

Whisk thoroughly to incorporate.

JOE BUCK

Midnight Cowboy
Recipe: Bill Norris
313 E 6th St
Austin, TX 78701
(512) 843-2715
midnightcowboymodeling.com

"My favorite thing about the place is the front door. It's the original door from the brothel. It's solid steel and hearing the chaos outside then hearing it shut out by that door is amazing," Bill Norris told me. He's the brain child behind Midnight Cowboy and Alamo Drafthouse's cocktail program. He's also Austin's OG when it comes to cocktails, having overseen the first craft cocktail program in Austin at Fino. The door also has a sliding peep hole that's about 4'9" off the ground because the Madame was a very petite Asian lady. Let me explain. Midnight Cowboy used to be named Midnight Cowboy Modeling and used to be a place where you could get your suspect roughed up, if you know what I mean. It was a house of ill repute run by a petite Asian lady. Now, this reservation-only speakeasy is one of the most incredible cocktail bars in Texas. Pro tip: Ring the name of a famous Savoy bartender for access.

And don't worry... they gutted the place. But they kept the door.

Glassware: **Copper Mule Mug**
Garnish: **Lemon Wheel half-dusted with Cayenne**

- **1.5 oz Balcones Baby Blue**
- **.5 oz honey Dijon syrup**
- **.5 oz lemon juice**
- **Ginger beer**

1. Shake all but ginger beer.

2. Pour into mug, top with ginger beer and more ice, swizzle, then garnish.

7
FORTALEZA
FORTALEZA
49.2 % Alc. Vol
49 % Alc. Vol
50.4 % Alc. Vol
JOVEN
JOVEN
JOVEN
JOVEN

TEXAS Cocktails OUTSIDE Texas

If you want a cocktail with some Texas flair, you need to have one made by a Texan. It's as simple as that. Here are some places you can visit for a Texan-made cocktail.

HERBS & RYE

BARTENDER: MATT GRAHAM - AUSTIN

3713 W Sahara Ave
Las Vegas, NV 89102
(702) 982-8036
herbsandrye.com

Matt's been bartending for over 20 years and got his start in the bars on Dirty 6th. "It was also long before craft cocktails were a thing and it helps to remind me not to take things too seriously," he told me. When asked what he would make if someone asked for a Texas cocktail, he said, "I'd throw it out there that I'd whip them up a delicious cocktail using a fresh Bluebonnet-Flower Syrup. Hopefully they'd get the joke since we all grew up believing that it is illegal to pick Bluebonnets off the side of the roads in Texas. I would then make them something along the lines of a whiskey sour or margarita which would hit the spot on a hot summer day."

EVANGELINE

BARTENDER: MICHAEL ANDERSON - LUBBOCK

453 Boulevard of the Allies
Pittsburgh, PA 15219
(412) 339-1870
distrikthotel.com

I met Michael at the St. Charles Exchange in Louisville and within two minutes, we were talking about Texas. That's what you do when you're Texan. He told me that Texas' world-class citrus and approach to food, whether its roasting, charring, or using peppers to bring some heat into the drinks, has impacted the way he builds his menus. He told me, "Texas screams tequila and mezcal at me. If asked, I would steer them in the direction of a margarita or paloma, something with agave."

SAXON + PAROLE

BARTENDER: KIP MOFFITT - HOUSTON

316 Bowery
New York, NY 10012
(212) 254-0350
saxonandparole.com

"My time in Texas has definitely built my career," Kip told me. "It was great working in the Montrose/RiverOaks area since 2005 and seeing all the new bars and restaurants pop up with influences from all over the world." Then we chatted a bit about how Texas has come into its own and created a distinct flavor. He said his version of a Texas cocktail starts with a Paloma, which is perfect. Regarding our home state ingredients, he said, "Texas gets such great citrus and has the best peppers. I didn't appreciate how incredibly flavorful Texas grapefruits were until I was in New York. The spicy peppers aren't spicy up here."

TEARDROP LOUNGE

Bartender: Nicolas Flower - Dallas

1015 NW Everett St
Portland, OR 97209
(503) 445-8109
teardroplounge.com

Nick got his start bartending in NYC but Texas culture has certainly had an impact on the way he approaches the work. "Ultimately, bartending is about hospitality. Where would I be without my parents and grandparents instilling that sense of warmth, friendliness, and generosity? There's never been a Thanksgiving dinner at our house where Mommaw didn't have it under control. I find that comforting and try to replicate it at the bar. Everyone can relax, we've got you," he told me. As for what a Texas cocktail is to him? Frozen margarita.

THE WALK IN

Bartender: Phillip Smith - Austin

2727 N Milwaukee Ave,
Chicago, IL 60647
www.thewalkinchicago.com

"To me, the most quintessentially Texas cocktail would be a Paloma. Agave based, Texas grown grapefruit, and perfect on a hot day... What else could you want in a Texas cocktail?" Phillip told me. This Austin native has moved to the Windy City to ply his craft, but the Texan roots still shine through. "Being from Texas has taught me genuine hospitality. It's what I really focus hard on with my new bar team. Genuinely caring about my guests when they walk in the door. It's just of second nature. I think it's in our blood." Go see him in Logan Square.

AMARO LUCANO
1894
LUCANIA
FERNET - LAZZARONI
AMARO
Since 1894
R. JELÍNEK
Original Recipe
FERNET
LIQUEUR
38 % ALC./VOL.
FERNET-VALLET
PRODUCTO DE MEXICO
FERNET-BRANCA
DARK WAS THE NIGHT
1 Blackstrap
.5 Lime
.5 VANILLA SYRUP
Soda

–INDEX–

—PHOTO CREDITS—

Photos by Nico Martini: pages 48, 51, 52, 56, 59, 60, 62-63, 70, 74, 81, 89, 93, 99, 100, 115, 123, 125, 141, 151, 173, 184, 191, 199. 200, 202, 204, 214, 221, 223, 224, 226, 227, 235, 243, 249, 254, 267, 268, 270, 323, 333, 345, 347, 350-351. Pages 1 and 34: courtesy of Chris Bostick and Claire McCormack Photography; pages 9 and 154: courtesy of Javier Flores; pages 10 and 162: courtesy of Brianna Balducci for Star Chefs; page 17: courtesy of Gina Kirkwood, New Waterloo; pages 22, 30, and 31: courtesy of Mark McDavid; page 32: courtesy of Voyageur Press and Emma Janzen; pages 33 and 69: courtesy of Max Walshe; pages 40, 67, 253, 257, and 259: courtesy of Kody Melton; pages 44-45 and 79: courtesy of SungJoon Koo; page 77: courtesy of Mark Koelsch; pages 82-83, 86, 107, 352, and 356-357: courtesy of Julie Soefer Photography; pages 90 and 93: courtesy of Whitmeyer's Distilling Co., Houston, TX; page 97: courtesy of Rich Bailey; page 104: courtesy of Kristen Gyorfi; page 111: courtesy of Houston Farris, Head Distiller; page 117: courtesy of Steven Salazar; page 127: courtesy of Jessica Sanders, drink.well.; pages 128 and 131: courtesy of Tito's Handmade Vodka; Page 139: Still Austin Whiskey Co.; page 143: courtesy of Revolution Spirits by Miguel Lecuona; page 144: courtesy of Amanda Turner; page 148: courtesy of Mike Groener; page 152: courtesy of Justin Lavenue and Dennis Gobis; page 158: courtesy of Small Victory; page 160: courtesy of SoCo Ginger Beer; page 165: courtesy of Nate Powell; page 167: courtesy of Mark Weatherford; pages 168-169 and 200: courtesy of Tony Alvarez; page 172: courtesy of Jones Long; page 175: courtesy of Jared Norton; page 176: courtesy of Chad Yarbrough; page

179: courtesy of Western Son Distillery; page 180: courtesy of Lauren Gebhardt, Bottled in Bond Cocktail Parlour and Kitchen; page 183: courtesy of Tawn Carranza; page 186: courtesy of Cowtown Paparazzi; page 193: courtesy of Chris Dempsey, D&D Shrubs and Syrups Co.; page 195: courtesy of Clark Cabus Photography; page 197: courtesy of Herman Marshall; page 205: courtesy of Edgar Campbell; pages 206 and 209: courtesy of Firestone & Robertson Distilling Co.; page 210: courtesy of Eric Pulido, Paschall Bar; page 214: courtesy of Amber Davidson, Bird Café; page 219: courtesy of Omar YeeFoon; pages 222 and 358: courtesy of Courtney Bradford; page 231: courtesy of Brad Hensarling, The Usual; pages 232, 236, and 263: courtesy of Front Burner Restaurants; pages 238-239, 264, and 266: courtesy of Hilmy Creative; pages 244 and 292: courtesy of Jason Risner Photography; pages 252 and 255: courtesy of Josh Huskin; page 270: courtesy of Azar Distilling; page 273: courtesy of Jonathan Rogers; page 278: courtesy of Black Pearl; page 281: courtesy of Alina Mikos & Mary Ellen "Mellen" Julsen; pages 283 and 285: courtesy of Deux South Creative; page 289: courtesy of Metropolitan; page 291: courtesy of Dripping Springs; pages 295 and 297: courtesy of Laura Merrian; page 299: courtesy of Christi Brinkman; page 300: courtesy of Manda Levy; page 302: courtesy of Justin Bowers, Captiv Creative; page 305: courtesy of Dan Garrison; page 308: courtesy of Daniel Copado; page 311: courtesy of Roberto Gonzalez, Tabernilla—Bar de Tapas, Laredo, TX; pages 312 and 313: courtesy of Stephanie Houston; page 317: courtesy of Ash Compton; page 318: courtesy of Erica Mann; page 323: courtesy of Bobby Gallagher/Lens Hungry/TradeCraft; page 324: courtesy of Alexandra Chabek (@7angerine); pages 326-327, 336, 337, and 339: courtesy of Juliet Beletic, EJB Creative; page 330: courtesy of Mongoose Vs Cobra; page 334: courtesy of Truck Yard; page 340: courtesy of Austin Marc Graff; page 343: courtesy of Beth Smith; page 348: courtesy of Tracy Rowland.

All other images used under official license from Shutterstock.com.

—ABOUT THE AUTHOR—

Born and raised in Texas, Nico Martini lives in Dallas with his wife, Sarah, and two sons Beckett and Declan. He is the Co-Founder of Grayson Blended Texas Bourbon, as well as Bar Draught, mobile draught cocktail solutions. He has presented at numerous industry events, including San Antonio Cocktail Conference, Tales of the Cocktails, Catersource, Portland Cocktail Week, and the Distilled Spirits Council of the United States Conference. His second book with Cider Mill Press, *Texas Whiskey*, was released in July 2021.

Martini is also a former Guest Lecturer at the University of Texas at Dallas, and prior to his transition to spirits he was a Program Director and on-air talent for CBS Radio's Indie-verse 100.3 HD2 in Dallas, performed in wild west comedy gunfight shows, and was a member of the Lincoln Center Director's Lab. He received, but didn't accept, a hockey scholarship to Penn State and recently gave a TEDx talk on cocktails. All of these statements are true, and yes, Martini is his legal last name.

–About Cider Mill Press Book Publishers–

Good ideas ripen with time. From seed to harvest, Cider Mill Press brings fine reading, information, and entertainment together between the covers of its creatively crafted books. Our Cider Mill bears fruit twice a year, publishing a new crop of titles each spring and fall.

CIDER MILL PRESS
BOOK PUBLISHERS

"Where Good Books Are Ready for Press"

501 Nelson Place
Nashville, Tennessee 37214

cidermillpress.com

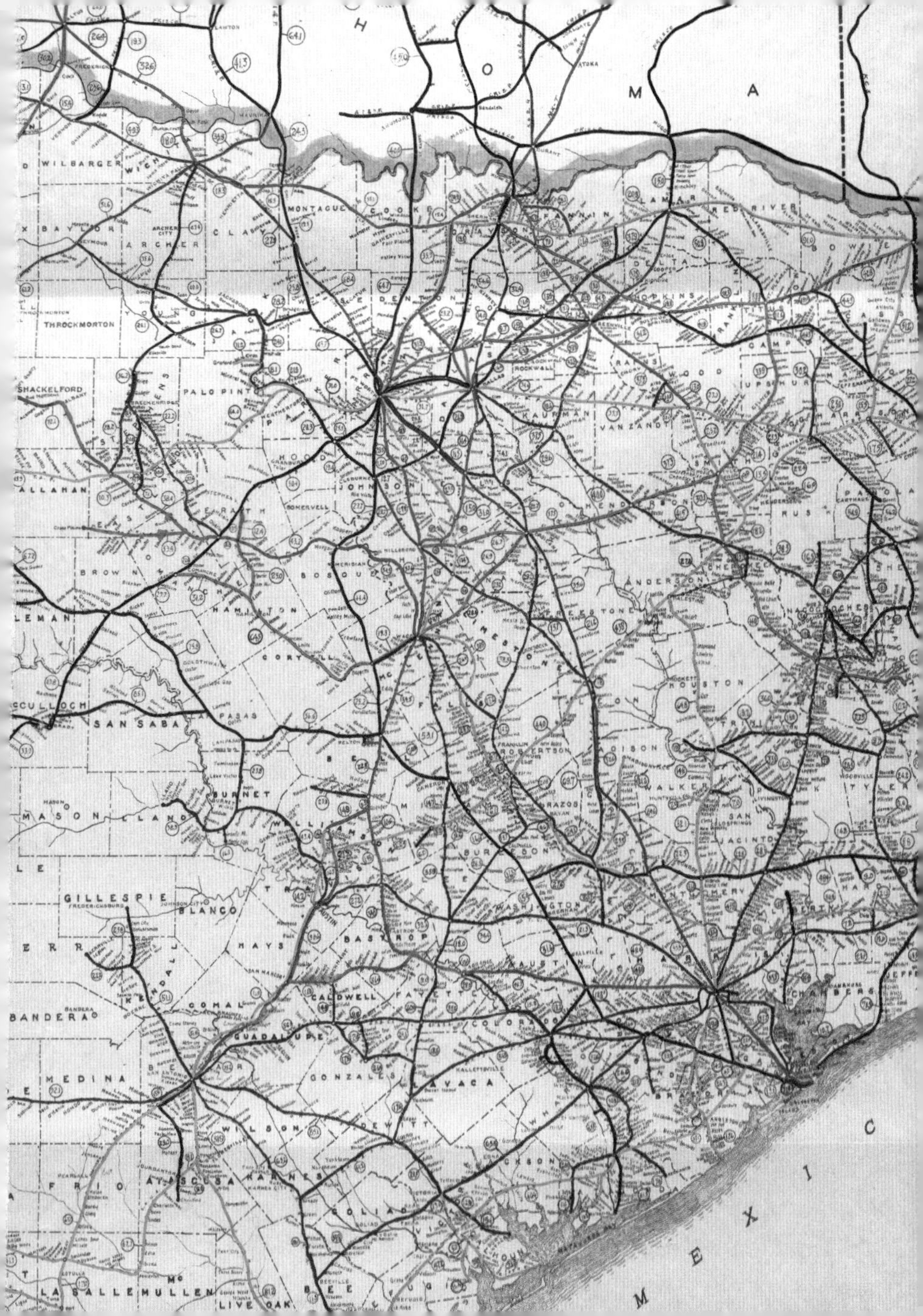
WILBARGER
BAYLOR
ARCHER
MONTAGUE
COOKE
LAMAR
RED RIVER
THROCKMORTON
SHACKELFORD
PALO PINTO
ROCKWALL
KAUFMAN
VAN ZANDT
UPSHUR
SOMERVELL
BROWN
HAMILTON
CORYELL
ANDERSON
FREESTONE
HOUSTON
SAN SABA
ROBERTSON
BURNET
MASON
LLANO
WALKER
SAN JACINTO
GILLESPIE
BLANCO
HAYS
BASTROP
CALDWELL
COMAL
BANDERA
GUADALUPE
MEDINA
GONZALES
LAVACA
WILSON
KARNES
GOLIAD
CHAMBERS
LA SALLE
MULLEN
LIVE OAK
BEE

PARMER
CASTRO
SWISHER
BRISCOE
HALL
BAILEY
LAMB
HALE
FLOYD
MOTLEY
COCHRAN
HOCKLEY
LUBBOCK
CROSBY
DICKENS
YOAKUM
TERRY
LYNN
GARZA
KENT
STONEWALL
GAINES
DAWSON
BORDEN
SCURRY
FISHER
ANDREWS
MARTIN
HOWARD
MITCHELL
NOLAN
LOVING
WINKLER
ECTOR
MIDLAND
GLASSCOCK
STERLING
COKE
CULBERSON
WARD
CRANE
UPTON
REAGAN
IRION
TOM GREEN
REEVES
SCHLEICHER
JEFF DAVIS
PECOS
CROCKETT
SUTTON
TERRELL
PRESIDIO
BREWSTER
VAL VERDE
EDWARDS
KINNEY
MAVERICK
ROSWELL
CARLSBAD
SAN ANGELO
2330
YELLOW
East Texas & Gulf Ry.
Groveton, Lufkin & Northern Ry.
Missouri Pacific Lines:
Asherton & Gulf Ry.
Beaumont, Sour Lake & Western Ry.
Houston & Brazos Valley Ry.
International-Great Northern R.R.
Orange & Northwestern R.R.
Rio Grande City Ry.
San Antonio, Uvalde & Gulf R.R.
St. Louis, Brownsville & Mexico Ry.
Sugar Land Ry.
Moscow, Camden & San Augustine Ry.
Texas & Pacific R.R.
Denison & Pacific Suburban Ry.
Texas Southeastern R.R.
Weatherford, Mineral Wells & Northwestern Ry.
ORANGE
Angelina & Neches River R.R.
Denison, Bonham & New Orleans R.R.
Fort Worth & Denver City Ry.
Texas City Terminal Ry.
Texas Midland R.R.
Trinity & Brazos Valley Ry.
BROWN
Chicago, Rock Island & Gulf Ry.
Eastland, Wichita Falls & Gulf R.R.
Nacogdoches & Southeastern R.R.
Paris & Mt. Pleasant R.R.